Croydon Beacl

Croydon Beach

_____

and more curious tales

Jeff Fountain

Jeff-Fountain.net

Croydon Beach

Also by Jeff Fountain

Like a James Dean Cigarette
A novel
Even Continents Drift
Short Stories

Croydon Beach

Published by Jeff fountain at Amazon
Copyright 2021 Jeff Fountain

This book which is the copyrighted property of the author. The work contained herein should not be reproduced without permission of the author for any commercial use.

All characters are fictitious and no similarity to any person alive or deceased should be implied

Please note that there are very occasional uses of language that may cause offence.

Cover Art: **FlapCat Design**

Croydon Beach

Acknowledgements

Once again I am particularly grateful to Josie and David Dwyer for their help in offering some valid criticisms, helpful suggestions and encouragement throughout.

Also to Maggie Brady for her forbearance in having to read through repeatedly for errors, corrections, omissions and typos. (The many of which that surely remain are solely my responsibility and for which I apologise.)

Thanks also go in part also to Covid 19 for keeping me tied to this writing machine.

Croydon Beach

Dedications

To my fine Americans this small book is dedicated.

Roger W, Cindi P-W, Theresa and Steve S.

You enriched me, thank you.

Contents

Crossing the Rubicon	9
Wealth	21
The Donkey Path	22
B – Attitude	37
The Daze of Pearly Spencer	41
Ashes to Ashdod	60
Croydon Beach	69
Light Blue Paper and Retire	84
The Fairy Godfather	105
The Renaissance of Rennie Sutcliffe	121
Mr Jeffers Dreams his Build House	131
The Bookseller's Temptation	146
Beggar's Belief – Small Change	157

Croydon Beach

Birds were talking.

One bird said to Billy Pilgrim.

'Poo-tee-weet, Poo-tee-weet'?

Slaughterhouse 5 – Vonnegut

Croydon Beach

Croydon Beach

Crossing the Rubicon

Ah have to tell you this tale about The Rubicon; not the Julius Caesar one in Italy, why no man! This Rubicon was a working men's club in Jarrow; and that's not pronounced the same way as posh Harrow down south mind. Nah; it's Jarra. Where's Jarra? It's at the centre of the world in the North East of England, near Newcastle, and it can proudly boast a lot of fine inhabitants. Sometimes they are called Geordies. You might well have heard of them. Well, this story is about a canny lad called Peter Desmond who came to grief this one night at the club. It's legend up here, though but. It took place way back in '74, when there was still some shipyards, steelworks, and all kinds of factories and men working in them. And hard working men needed a working man's pastime now, didn't they?

Right, so this night it all started, Peter Desmond could not have wanted for a better end to the evening, everything was going great. For a week previous he'd worried himself awake trying to figure all the ways it could go wrong. But nothing did go wrong, he'd thought of everything. His first Saturday night at The Ruby Working Mens Club as entertainment secretary was a success; for the first time *he* was a success. At the edge of the stage he drank it all in. The final act was on stage and she was going down well with the audience. The music throbbed and there in the spotlight The Lovely Lesley swayed her way through her routine teasing items of costume from her body. That Lesley was real special alright, and somehow different.

Croydon Beach

Confidence began to well in him.

Peter ground out his last cigarette. Tonight, he thought to himself, he would definitely give up smoking. Through the dissipating smoke Peter examined the audience again, feeling their tension and expectation. He knew what they were thinking and it was him who'd put those thoughts there. For the first time in his life he felt in control, he had direction, he had power.

As Lesley languorously explored the small stage in her pool of light, Peter's eyes moved to the front tables and studied their occupants at length. He was enjoying the moment, his moment. Suddenly a face stabbed out at him from the semi-gloom, and like a gunfighter sensing danger in a crowded saloon, he reached automatically for his packet of tabs. He pulled one roughly from the pack and without taking his eyes from that face, jammed it into his mouth and lit it. His moment was gone. His head dropped to his chest and silent words smoked from his mouth.

'Aw Mam, what are *you* doing here?'

A familiar foreboding overtook Peter as he looked at his mother sitting expressionless amongst the quiet excitement, staring at her son. He felt like a child once again and about to be punished for some unremembered sin. It just wasn't fair.

Jenny Desmond's presence, was like a ghost at the feast, presaging something sinister. Tonight was going to be special alright and not just for Peter. The Ruby was never going to be the same again.

*

Now the Rubicon Working Men's club or just The Ruby as it's known 'round here in Jarra was much the same as any other working men's club on Tyneside or the North East for that matter. The beer's the same, there's snooker and darts and there's bingo every Monday and Thursday. But things started to change, and change irrevocably that time Jenny Desmond first set foot in the place. Up to that time she had solemnly vowed never to be seen there while her husband Matty was alive. But since his death from beer, gambling, premature idleness and fishing, common levellers in the North East, she had been as curious as a spaniel's nose to find out what exerted such a pull on the men thereabouts. A pull mind, that Matty had successfully failed to resist in twenty-nine years of marriage and even before that. And in common with all successful men, failure was not a word he understood. Another was moderation.

'I'm away to The Ruby for a wet, hinny.' Matty called from the hall. It was Sunday again and as usual he oozed well rehearsed anticipation. Years of unrelenting liver abuse had waxed his congenitally sallow complexion. The constant drink and the day's shave had put an artificial redness to his hollow cheeks making him look uncannily like a collapsing plastic apple. 'Just off for a couple, pet, OK?' It wasn't a question of course, but the same Sunday liturgical chant repeated throughout the estate.

'Righto, Matty. Now don't be late.' Was the usual unheeded response.

Once and only once out of casual curiosity she'd asked; 'Have ya ever thought of giving up the drink, Matty? For a while like, y'know?'

It was a redundant question of course and Jenny knew it. But it passed some time while she strung beans for the weekly roast into the kitchen sink. Matty wouldn't claim to be a religious man but to him as with many others, Sunday was a sacred day and the merest hint of missing lunchtime doors was something on the far side of sacrilegious. Caught briefly in the hall by the question, like a diver in an air-lock, he idly explored the pockets of his best top coat as if searching for an answer, eyes still fixed on the front door knob.

'I'll tell ya Pet,' he'd call back, 'thinking has sent more men to hell than a belly full of beer. I'll see yez later.' And the draught at Jenny's neck would tell her that he was away, happy in the knowledge of his own salvation.

It was three Sundays after Matty died and while still stringing enough beans for the two of them, she'd made up her mind to find out what it was about The Ruby that made her such a demanding mistress. She'd received a letter a few days before from the club committee offering condolences for her loss and assuring her that she was always welcome at The Ruby.

'Alright, alright, I'll sign ya in.' Jenny's son Peter was not at all happy about his mother going to the club. Outside the entrance he finally gave up and gave in. 'Have it your own way as usual. But you're not with me, OK? Whatever happens, ah don't want to know.' He signed Jenny and her friend Nancy, another initiate, in, then disappeared faster than a shipyard vacancy, so fast, in fact, he forgot to tell his mother one important detail.

In daylight the club looked nothing special, just a flat roofed utility building, its walls blinded by huge plate windows; a couple of Federation Ales adverts outside, and a pair of robust double doors leading the way in. But at night it was different. At night you could see its lights streets away, bouncing off the vapour clouds from the coke works. When darkness fell, The Ruby looked like the spaceship from Close Encounters had landed off-course right in the middle of the Scotch Housing Estate. It was magic.

Inside Jenny and Nancy stood in the focus of the main foyer and looked at the various rooms radiating from its heart. The foyer

Croydon Beach

was brightly illuminated by fluorescent strip lights which made the heavy floral wallpaper turn autumnal. The ceiling was finished off in white with a heavy hint of cork-tipped smoke the colour of old chip shop oil. Jenny distracted Nancy from her reverie. Nancy was a small woman who never seemed sure about anything. Just now she looked like a kid queuing for her first Waltzer ride in Spanish City.

'Er, what did you say, Pet?'

'Ah said, where do you fancy, Nancy? Which bar?'

'Ee, well I don't know, I'm sure.' Nancy would follow Jenny anywhere. I'm sure, was Nancy's favoured expression, and seemed to follow almost every utterance.

'How about the lounge then?'

'If you think we should.'

In they went, found seats and Jenny insisted on buying the drinks. They were getting looks from all around.

'Look at us Jenny, both of us recently widowed and getting the once over from the local wasters. We'll be alright tonight,' she joked.

They weren't.

Half an hour later they were on their way home, with Jenny erupting curses and threats to various anatomical parts of men in general and the particular bits of the barman who had just refused to serve them. Nancy was sure she had never heard such language from her old friend before. Jenny kept running the scene through her head so as to keep the momentum of her anger. She didn't want it to let it pass into reasoned inertia. She still couldn't believe what she'd heard.

There she had stood at the bar with money in her outstretched hand as the shards of a shattered smile fell from her lips.

'I beg your pardon? What did you say?'

But the barman was gone and Jenny was left standing staring at the space where he had been. Her jaw was open, her eyes wide and seemingly fixed on the last tired meat pie resting in its perspex aquarium.

'We're very particular who we serve here, pet,' the barman said, returning. Not looking at her mind, but speaking as he pulled pints for another round.

'This not a pub ya know, it's a club. For men y'see.' The beer frothed excitedly into the glasses. He leaned over closer to Jenny and rejoined; 'A *men's* club.' This he said with that special matter-of-fact emphasis which North-Eastern men reserve for when answering unasked questions. Such as when presenting their sweethearts with flowers or observing equally rare heavenly phenomena. 'Why, they're flowers', they might say, or 'That's Haley's Comet, that is'. Impressed with his revelation the barman rocked back on certain ground and in a louder and more certain voice added, 'And there's nay point in standing there, you wont get served and that's that.'

Jenny wasn't one to let it go at that.

'Are you telling me that you are not going to serve me drinks in this club just because.....'

Oliver had kept bar at the Rubicon Club for thirteen years and had dealt with this several times. He was Tyneside's sarcastic stress expert.

'That's right pet, because you are a woman. That's the rule. And like I say, you can stand there 'til Sunderland win the European cup and gets itself a Conservative MP, ya still won't get served. So get yourself a man and you can have a drink, but not before.' And with that he turned his back and continued lining up pints of Scotch bitter with heads like over-soaped babies.

Jenny glanced up at the man who had just ordered the beer. He split his whiskers and threw Jenny a grin, but she was too quick for him and intercepted the pass.

Croydon Beach

'Don't bother bonny lad, a'd rather hang meself.'

And the grin disappeared back into the unshaven face.

'Where's the drinks then Jenny, where've you been?' asked Nancy, as Jenny returned to their table.

'You'll never believe this Nancy, I couldn't get served.'

Nancy frowned. 'What ja mean?'

'He said I was a woman.'

'Why that's a bit obvious isn't it?'

'No, no, he said I couldn't get served *because* I was a woman.'

'Ee, he never did.' Nancy looked more confused.

'We are going to see about this. Come on Nancy.'

'Oh no. Can't we just go to the pub instead and forget about it.' Nancy could not stand trouble and she instinctively knew this was trouble.

'Jenny, the pub, eh, come on? I'm sure it'll blow over.'

It wouldn't and Jenny was making the smoke of a Tyneside built Class Seven destroyer and was gone, Nancy in tow.

*

'Look, Mam, I'll say this once again.' Peter rubbed his face vigorously with hands that were meant for riveting ships together, but since leaving school had been employed persuading luke warm burgers between the lips of limp sesame buns, as jobs were starting to disappear from the yards. This had been the fourth time he'd tried to explain the rules of the working men's club and frustration was beginning to sneak past his usually placid demeanour. He took a breath and had another rush at explaining.

'Mam, The Rubicon Working Men's Club is a working men's club right? It clearly states the fact that it's for blokes right?'

Croydon Beach

Jenny scowled at Peter. 'So?'

'Right. So only men are allowed to be members right?' Jenny sighed. 'Now then,' continued Peter trying to remember why he'd started all this. If it wasn't for the fact that he was recently elected entertainments secretary, he would just have said I told ya so, and make no attempt to explain the cause of his mother's public humiliation. 'Only members are allowed to buy drinks, so…' He cut Jenny off before she interrupted. 'So, because only men can be members, only men can buy drinks. See?' Impressed with the clarity and logic of the explanation Peter sat back sure that his mother understood this time.

She understood alright, in fact she understood only too well. She seemed placated, but the next gratuitous remark stirred her back into rage.

'There's nothing you can do about it, but you can always get blokes ta buy ya drinks for ya if ya want. Ah just don't see the problem.'

As soon as it was out of his mouth he regretted it and knew this wouldn't end it and a tiredness began to leech into his brain.

'You don't, eh? Well, I'll tell you what the problem is.' Anger rose in Jenny like Yorkshire pudding in a hot oven, as Peter resisted a need to sigh loudly. 'I'll tell you alright, bonny lad. If The Rubicon is, as you say it is, a working men's club how come most of the *men* who get in there haven't worked since beer came off ration? Tell me that. It's us women who do the work around here. You're just the same as the rest of them. Your mother's shown up in front of a bunch of witless ne'r-do-wells at that club of yours, and you apologise for them!' Her anger was just in check.

'I don't work then, is that right? Is that what you're saying?'

'If you can call that work.'

Croydon Beach

It was an old wound Peter didn't want opened up and so let it go. He had become entangled in his own logical string that he couldn't unravel.

'Mam, for the last time…' But he had failed and he knew it. It was impossible to argue with his mother, he'd tried it before. Women were a different species and didn't understand the burdens men are doomed to carry through this life. His dad had been right.

'Son, one piece of advice.' It was Peter's eighteenth birthday and his very first legal round at The Ruby, 'Life is a horse race with only one direction. You start as a stallion and that's the way you want to pass the post. You want to end up a gelding, then start trying to understand women.' His father lifted his glass carefully appreciating its contents like a diamond merchant at his work and continued his sporting metaphor. 'They're your hurdles son, jump 'em, but for God's sake don't fall. So here's to your first furlong. Cheers.' And his father downed the pint in three swallows, leaving a frothy moustache slowly dissipating as he ordered two more.

Yep, dad had been right. Men were men and women weren't. That was that.

'Mam, There's nothing you can do about it, he repeated. 'So what's the point?'

As Peter left for the club that evening, he had the certain feeling that his mother wouldn't leave it at that. He would be in for more of the same sooner or later and began re-examining his decision not to emigrate South. These feelings would of course soon evaporate as they always had once the first swallowing mouthfuls of Forty Shilling ale hit his stomach; it was forgotten.

Jenny did not forget so easily. Jenny was the type who persisted and didn't give in to the sanguine fatalism of the North-eastern male. Not for her the unravelling of the legal framework of discrimination and inequality. No. For Jenny it was always action. She had been the one who had kept the family together ever since Matty Jesmond no sooner had their son been born, than he'd lost his job as a riveter at the ship yards. She had cajoled him into finding other jobs, but they'd lasted no longer than a greyhound's sprint. He wasn't a lazy man, he was just tired of the chase, tired of trying, tired. So she stopped asking and got on with the part time jobs and going without so that Peter would have a fair crack. Here he was, a good lad after his father in his father's image. In the North-East it seemed, it was the women who drove; men were driven. Jenny had decided upon a plan. She didn't have one yet, but she wouldn't let that stop her.

'Nancy, I have a plan,' she told her friend conspiratorially. After a few days of angry contemplation.

'A plan? A plan for what?' Nancy hunched her disproportionately large shoulders. 'A plan for what?'

'About what happened the other day, in The Ruby.'

'Oh, do you not think it's best left alone. I'm sure it would be only causing more trouble.'

Jenny ignored her friend's caution and carried on explaining her plan.

'Listen, Nancy. You know our Peter's the club's entertainments secretary, and you know how I'm always tidying up after him?. Well, look what I found - his little work phone book... '

As the plan was told, Nancy knew that she would not be able to talk Jenny out of it. She just didn't want anything to do with it. Jenny would have to go it alone.

Saturday night at The Ruby was variety entertainment night. On a

Croydon Beach

typical night there could be a conjurer, a ventriloquist, <u>mebbies</u> a sing-song or a comic. As was the custom, the wives and or girlfriends were allowed out with their men to watch somebody else's wife or girlfriend take her clothes off to the pulsing rhythms of catcalls and whistling.

This would be Peter's finest hour. He had arranged a full evening's entertainment and was as nervous as a box of giveaway kittens. After announcing the final act of the evening – The Lovely Lesley all the way from Seaton Sluice, he stepped back out of the spotlight. It was then his eyes picked out his mother in the front row, staring fixedly straight at her son, and foreboding began to nibble away at his hard won confidence.

Lesley came on and she was a real looker. Men were gulping audibly and concentrating completely on their own thoughts and the erotic spectacle unrobing before them. That Lesley really was something special, no amateur she. She knew how to work the room, and every man in it. Jenny wasn't looking at The Lovely Lesley or at Peter, she was looking at the men, enjoying the moment. There was Oliver behind the bar shouting encouragement; there was whiskers, his eyes shining above his two pints. Perhaps, Peter thought in a moment of hope, he needn't worry, it was going so well. The fact that the agency had sent a different act at the last minute had concerned him at first, but this surely would prove to be his finest hour. Everyone was enjoying The Lovely Lesley; Peter faced it, he was a success.

As Lesley's sequinned body swayed sinuously to the throbbing rhythms and the finale approached, the men in the room were as one; silent, swallowing hard as they concentrated on what was happening before their eyes. Lesley turned, and with her back to the room, slowly removed the last vestiges, then spun back one-hundred and eight degrees…! making a large and full frontal X on the stage, at the very moment the music abruptly stopped. Perfection. Then a beer glass smashed somewhere, and the room was deathly silent. Jenny's eyes flashed to the men, then to Peter. All were a picture, a picture worth a several thousand words.

In the silence, Lesley's finale pose was slowly melting from the sky-scraping X to a forlorn why. This was not the reception The Lovely Lesley was expecting. Alone, Jenny stood and applauded.

'Never mind, pet,' she called to the luckless Lesley in the silence, 'I thought you were great. Why don't ya go and buy yourself a drink, and get me one while you're at it.'

Croydon Beach

Wealth

A man of limited means is walking in the woods
and finds a discarded pair of boots.
They are old and careworn; the laces slippery from rain.
Inside mould grows

He looks at the soles and they are sound.
The stitching of the uppers holding – fast.
The only shine is the one they have for the old man.

He looks at his own boots, about the same size.
Yes, try them.
He eases his feet from their fetid enclosures
and slips them easily into the found pair.
Perfect – the glove of boots.
He smiles.

He considers his old boots
They have been with him many years and many miles
It feels like betrayal.
Not with standing, he leaves them in the place he found his new
ones and happily goes his way.
....

A man of limited means is walking in the woods,
And finds a discarded pair of boots.
They are old and careworn, the laces slippery from rain,
Inside mould grows.

Croydon Beach

The Donkey Path

'We are outside the house of Dr Denzil Starke, who today, after a long period of silence is finally to speak on his removal from the Chair of History at Boleyn College, Cambridge, following the comments attributed to him regarding the Black Lives Matter's slavery and slave trade controversy and Britain's central role in it. He has seen his forthcoming book, 'Henry VIII and The First Brexit', withdrawn from his publishers list. In the book he posits the view that Henry the Eighth, broke with Rome in 1533 for the same reasons the UK abandoned the treaty of Rome in 2016. and I quote: "We may be poorer, but we have our freedom," he insists, "And that will be worth it."

'Other history academics have pointed out what he doesn't say in his book: Henry's schism with the catholic church led to long wars with catholic Spain and France and a fall in the wealth, power and influence of the English realm. Might the same be said of our withdrawal from the EU..?

Wait, here he is about to speak live outside his home. Dr Denzil Starke.'

'Thank you. I shall read this prepared statement and following it shall not be taking questions.

'I am a gay man. In the 1960s, when it was still against the law to show your affection to and for a man that you love, I stood and fought for what I believed was right. I campaigned for those rights which have since become enshrined in British law. I am not a bigot, a racist, history denier, or homophobe, how could I be? I am an

Croydon Beach

historian, with truth as my guiding light and principle. And yet it seems that if one speaks the truth… If one speaks the truth, as one sees it and has studied it over many years, one is vilified and pursued by elements in this country who will tarnish our precious thousand year old jewel – the freedom to speak.

'I know then what it is to be an outcast. I am also a white man, an Englishman and find myself internally banished within our Kingdom; shunned; a pariah. This was my fate. And why? Why, because of a few deliberately misinterpreted words that have pursued and hounded me.

'Those views were spoken during a streamed political interview for a private, and yes, right of centre channel on the internet, and using a few perhaps clumsy sentences to express my firmly held views. These words have upset the so-called WOKE and BLM industrial complex including many others of the politically correct police who now flourish on the mainstream media. Yes, slavery is an awful thing and I have made that plain, but I merely expressed it in, shall we say a florid manner. I am no revisionist, I am an historian and therefore I will repeat them here: "Slavery was not genocide, otherwise there wouldn't be so many damn blacks in Africa or Britain would there? An awful lot of them survived?" It is a view and one which I firmly stand by.

'So, be warned Britain, the WOKE PC police are coming for you. That is all I have to say.'

'Well, an unrepentant Dr Denzil Starke there, speaking live outside his home. This is Ejewo Okonkwo, for BBC News, Norwich.'

It is a fine summer's day on Italy's Calabrian coast and Denzil Starke finds himself alone hiking, hugging as closely as he can its rugged shore. His sixty-five years have not physically dulled his enthusiasm or his ability to climb and scale some of the tricky terrain, despite the way he has chosen being promoted as 'a tourist path'. He had decided on a solitary holiday wanting to be away from all the controversy of the moment. It's not that the Italians didn't care about the nonsense he was leaving behind, they had a different way of handling such things – they ignored it.

For his walking vacation, he had booked ahead various taverna and small hotels where he would find his luggage waiting for him at each stop, along with a good bed, showers and some fine local Italian cuisine. Starke strode confidently along, pushing all thoughts away and trying to be in the moment. The tension was slowly dissipating the further and longer he walked. Yet still, he could not shake off the injustice he so sorely felt in his ageing bones.

Here he was, emeritus history professor at a prestigious Cambridge college. He'd had two series on BBC on the Tudors, his historical oeuvre.

'Now I am pariah, an isolate, cast out by the WOKE revisionists and do-gooders, banished to the wilderness,' Starke fumed once more. 'I'm like Doré's Wandering Jew, who mocked Jesus on his way to crucifixion, condemned to walk the earth until the second coming. Hmm,' he thought, 'I hope I wont be wandering about that long!' He grinned at his own dark humour.

Oh yes, he knew those feelings of unjust persecution alright. And now, his new book would not be published and his agent had deserted him. He was tainted, and why? For a few words spoken on a private Youtube channel that had a viewership of less than thirty-thousand. At the time, the interview had felt intimate, as if he was talking in confidence to friends of his political constituency. He hadn't realised quite how it was that the lines he spoke, almost in confidence, could suddenly become instantly repeated outside that cosy little studio. It had gone viral and he had received some very nasty trolling messages as well as widespread coverage on all mainstream media.

Sure, he'd got his supporters, but they were not the kind of people he wanted to associate with; racists and far right parties, who would support him whatever he said from then on.

He had been ostracised by his peers, banished from the academic realm he had worked so hard to become an accepted part of. From his lowly origins he'd had to steel his resolve over many years to become a well regarded academician. It hadn't been easy. Raised in poverty by a doting mother who took in laundry, and communist father, who cleaned windows. Certainly Starke had previous form, particularly on BBC's Question Time and Radio Four's Any Questions, but he had always kept just this side of that uncrossable line, until now. Now he had crossed over there was no going back. He needed time to think and stiffen that resolve once more.

'Damn it all,' he said out loud as he rounded a headland and gazing down on the rocky shore below, 'how long will this last? Surely people will forget? At least they haven't barred me from the Moral Maze.' Five minutes later as he continued to stare at the sea a text appeared on his phone. It was from the producer of the Moral Maze, stating that he would not be on the next discussion programme as planned. 'Brilliant,' he said, a broad ironic grin disfiguring his face once more. 'Typical left wing BB bloody C.' The rest of the message continued: 'However, the subject will now focus upon the moral issues surrounding your statements on slavery and whether it was fitting to ban you from the university. We hope this will meet with your approval, if not your acceptance, as it will be about you and not with you, as you are still PNGrata here. As your erstwhile producer, I felt that I should let you know our plans. It is an ongoing hot topic of debate. Tamara P.' And that was that. He noted, with no surprise, that there were no expressions of regret at the turn of events.

Well, he supposed, at least they are looking at the right issues. He tried to console himself with what he knew of people and their tendency for memory lapse – people would forget, they always do, always did. That is how politician's promises that are never kept come back years later, reformed and represented and believed. People were like the comrades in Animal Farm, who couldn't remember what had been promised before and just went along with what their leaders said. 'People are pretty dumb,' he concluded, 'they forget so easily. I'll be back when memory fades, as it always does. People will forget, they always do.'

Starke would sometimes recall with a great deal of personal and professional satisfaction, a small incident on the Moral Maze when an eminent professor of Greek history was arguing that history is not fixed but open to interpretation as new research comes to light and which changed accepted ideas of the past. Starke profoundly disagreed with this view as revisionism of the most execrable kind. History, he contended does not have amnesia. It does not change, but is immutable and fixed. It is human recall that is faulty not the past itself.

Resurrecting these thoughts, The Doctor's notorious supercilious grin, melted into a confident smile. 'Yes, of course. I'll be back when the dust settles over the events and memory is buried and dead. I will not be silenced. It will all be a forgotten footnote of history.'

Still smiling, and sitting on a warm rock, Starke unpacked a

Croydon Beach

thermos from his small backpack, and poured himself a coffee, trying to be in the moment, and not think of the moment his partner walked out on him, just before he left for his vacation.

'My god,' Andrew had said, confronting Starke following the revelation of his slavery comments, 'you have said and done some pretty rotten things in your time, but that is just awful. You repeated it, uncontrite and this time to the world's press, like you were proud of what you said.'

'I was, I am,' assured Starke, resolutely. 'And I stand by it. Firm and sure. This is me, you know that. And now you are going that way of all WOKEs, running with the crowd, baying for blood to salve something you imagine could be your white liberal conscience.'

'And that's it, is it? No remorse, no compassion. I just cannot be with this or you any more. I'm sorry, I need some space away from you.' And by the end of the day he was gone.

Twenty three years together, and in that time they had their rows, which long term couples don't? This was different. Would Andrew ever forgive him, even though he felt not the slightest need to be forgiven. Would he, like the rest of humanity, forget? Of course; they always do – amnesia is a common condition of the masses.

The coffee finished, Starke screwed back the cap and then twisted the cup into it place, bagged it, stood and stretched readying himself for the last ten kilometres to his next lodging. He had plenty of time. As he stood, it was then, below him set high on the cliffside overlooking the sea, he noticed the squat spire of a church. He leaned over as far as he could without toppling and from what he could see, the church was perhaps no more than a chapel, painted bright white, and roofed with the classic mediterranean terracotta barrel clay tiles that adorned nearly every house along the coast and beyond.

Croydon Beach

'Where there's a church, there is history,' he said to himself excitedly. 'And a community, and just maybe a place for a spot of lunch.' He would look for an access route to the church and start exploring. Just what he needed right then, the enfolding arms of history's comfort. Here was Frost's Road Less Travelled, and it called to him.

Following the path he eventually found a well trodden track leading away and down toward the sea. There was no sign to announce the place, and when he consulted his map, and checked his phone's geo-locator he could find no mention of a settlement nearby.

'Interesting and intriguing,' he said aloud. 'Excellent. Let's see where it leads.'

The track followed an ancient donkey route. For hundreds of years before surveyors had laced every land with roads and highways, village paysans would define a treacherous hillside path by encouraging a mule or donkey to negotiate its own least difficult way. They knew that the animal would always try to find the easiest route and so they would follow marking the route as it climbed. Over time the donkey's path, not the most direct but the most accessible, would become the beaten and well trod way, followed unquestioningly, and until someone found a better way, it would do.

To Starke, it wasn't an easy path, and seemed little used. At the end of it he expected to find nothing but the abandoned church he had spied from above, but you never knew. About halfway down the cliff path almost stumbling to a fall, he rounded an awkward bend and there laid out before him, the most beautiful vista he had ever witnessed or could have possibly have imagined. It took his breath away. He stood utterly transfixed, marvelling at it.

Framed by a brilliant azure sky and clear blue Tyrrhenian Sea, was a miracle. He slowly lowered himself to sit and drink it in. Before

Croydon Beach

him was a small harbour with a hook of a breakwater sheltering a half a dozen small colourful fishing boats moored alongside the wall. Landward side, a flight of tidy houses rose up the gentle slopes towards the cliff, each painted white, glaring in the sunshine; only individually distinguished by the colour of the doors and windows, painted garish shades of red, blue and green. Perched on each of the tall chimneys, a common sight of the region, the untidy occupied heaps of Demoiselle cranes' nests, with the leggy birds strutting watchfully around their gawking offspring. Encouraged as symbols of good fortune, generations of these huge birds would, were they able, thought Starke, testify to their own long unbroken histories in this place. Behind and higher, under the cliff, nestled the small church, reached by a narrow dust path from the village that led worshipers to its services and salvation. Above the sea, that jewelled brilliantly under the early afternoon sun, skuas and jaegers wheeled about calling, squabbling or gracefully diving for fish.

The place appeared empty of souls. It was that time of day when sensible Calabrians took to their beds after a lunch of pasta, fish and wine. Perhaps to make love, certainly to rest until the cool evening breeze blew from the sea. He could see no vehicles. How would they get down and back? Was there no road? It seemed from first observations, there wasn't. There were no satellite dishes to scar the roof lines, no phone masts or cables strung untidily about and between the dwellings. It seemed to Starke that he had stumbled into a history of his own, a place frozen in time with no obvious associations with the present at all. He marvelled at it and he would explore.

It took him twenty minutes to finally find the start of what could amusingly be called the main street. The uneven cobbled way led quickly to the harbour on the right and to the tidy houses hard by

Croydon Beach

on the opposite side. He was disappointed to see there was no café, but the disappointment was soon overwhelmed by what he was experiencing. Where should he begin? Well, the harbour wall looked promising, from there he could get a view back to see the full panoramic beauty of the little fishing settlement.

The sound of the sea lapping the wall and rocking the boats at their mooring was a music he would never tire of, he felt sure. The boats plopped and sucked, rose and gently fell with the small swell that the light breeze stirred within the harbour's sanctuary. He walked towards the end of the wall and turned to stare back, then spun on his heel, and with his eyes firmly closed and facing the village opened them, and there it was. In the foreground the boats, moving rhythmically, birds wheeling above, calling. Behind, the modest tidy houses, stepped up the cliff towards the church. If he could have framed it, taken it back with him, he would have. Memory and a few phone pictures would have to suffice.

It was then a deep bronchial cough shattered the peace. Something disgusting was hawked up and spat. Starke turned. There, not three metres along the wall with his feet hanging over the very end of the harbour wall, was a man he hadn't noticed. It seemed he was concentrating very hard on smoking a short stub of a cigarette that he pinched between thick fingers, almost certainly scorching their tips. The man had about him the look of someone wholly exhausted with life and all its tribulations; his body was slumped forward, his whole demeanour exuding a misery and melancholy with whatever troubled him. At least so it seemed to Starke. He could not believe that someone who lived in such an idyll could be forlorn with his place in the world.

'Perhaps if I told him my woes he would cheer up a bit,' thought Starke, 'it might throw his own into sharp relief.' Then again

Croydon Beach

maybe he should leave this man to his personal purgatory. But after a short while the man's mood began to be transmitted to the scene around Starke, infecting the light hearted mood with increasing gloom. He would have to move away from this Jeremiah with his miserable contagion. Then he thought, no, why should he? Maybe he would challenge him to take himself off somewhere else, away from this almost sacred place.

'*Mi scusi. Buongiorno signor,*' offered Starke in his limited Italian. But the man just carried on with his cigarette despite the pain in his scorching fingers he must surely be feeling. '*Stai bene?*'

Eventually the man looked up toward and through Starke, who could see sadness etched into his sun leathered face. He said nothing and went back to looking down into the sea. Starke wondered if perhaps the man was thinking of killing himself. 'That's all I need,' thought Starke. 'Here I am on a beautiful day, potentially spoiled by the selfish action of one individual.' Maybe he should just leave the man to his individual fate and Starke would tend to his?

'*Parla inglese?*' asked Starke. He always wondered about the inanity of asking a question like that. A question he could have asked in English and if he understood he would speak it. Never mind, it was the polite thing to do, he supposed.

The man took one final tight pull on his smoke and let the tiny cigarette end fall and extinguish in the otherwise clear blue sea, briefly polluting this perfect scene. The man rubbed his fingers against the leg of his grubby work clothes and turned his face to Starke and this time spoke. 'Little,' was all he managed. It was like pulling teeth, this man did not want company, either that or he was just not accustomed to it.

Starke managed with some stiffness to squat down on the wall a short distance away from the man, likewise hanging his feet over the edge, trying to establish common body language.

'*Signor, per favore*, can I ask... may I ask something?' Starke adjusted his sun hat so that his eyes were shaded and he could look at the man without squinting. He carried on without the man's permission and without his seeming interested in Starke's inquiry Being the sort of man Starke was; used, as he was to expecting to command attention from any chosen interlocutor, he plunged on with his question, trying to keep it as simple as he could. It did not occur to Starke that in someone else's country it would have been the thing to do, to at least try to converse in the native tongue. But being a Brexit Brit, even a well educated one, who chose to languish in the glories of England's history and the English language, for him, being stuck in his own language was no bad thing; indeed something to be treasured and celebrated. Long ago Starke had chosen to occupy England's past, making it his life's work; a past replete with faux memories and cheesecloth filtered recollections of a misty benevolent global Empire that spread the spirit of Christian capitalism, with its protestant ethic, through its industrial and military might. Jellied in a time, when Britain truly was a global nation, its past glories soon to be revived beyond the limiting confines of countries such as the one in which he found himself at that moment – albeit as the welcome guest. As he had once said, following the Brexit vote: 'If the United Kingdom wants a return to the past, then so be it. There is nothing, nothing in that past we have any reason to be ashamed of, or that I for one would not recall with pride. We have finally come to our senses.' The BBC Question time audience gave him a rousing cheer and long applause – Starke had found his country's zeitgeist – an unforgettable and unforgetting past.

'Can you tell me,' he said, dragging out the words for the foreigner along the wall, forgetting that it was he who was the foreigner, the outsider. 'Tell me why it is, that you find yourself in one of the most beautiful places I have ever seen in my life, it has everything, a place that has let modernity – I mean, modern life, pass by. Why it is that you look so unhappy, er, *perché... così triste?*'

Starke was truly bewildered and increasingly irritated by the wordless, rude and ungrateful man. If he had found himself in the English equivalent of this place untouched by so called progress, he would revel in it.

It took a while before the man gave any real indication that he was aware of Starke's question. Starke for his part couldn't be sure if this man was just the village imbecile incapable of communicating. He was about to leave the man to himself and his misery, rise and leave, getting a final and lasting look at this marvellous place, before deciding to try one more time to get his attention. '*Signor?*' he asked again. Still no reply. 'Enough then!' Starke stood, he wasn't used to being ignored and would not tolerate it, no *signor*! He stood, stiffly rising to his feet and turned his back on the man, to take one last long look at the village, when the man spoke.

'Much time ago I make to serve my village many ways I can.' said the gruff smokey voice, cracking as if it hadn't been used in the recent past. He coughed and again hawked unpleasantly into the pristine water. 'For eh… *quarant'anni*, my life, I give my time and my work to making things *bene*, er, good, for people here.' He paused and looked seaward, as if something was beckoning him out there, from some silent far off place beyond the shimmering horizon. 'But…ah!' He took a few deep breaths before continuing, a deep melancholy returned to his voice, heavy of course with accent, but fluent and articulate.. 'That church, on the hill,' the man continued.

'*Multo bello*, very beautiful!' interjected Starke.

'Yes, very beautiful,' repeated the man. '*Grazie*'. I tell you, it

Croydon Beach

was I, Luigi Gabrielli, build that church with my own hands,' he held them open, studying them, taking in their familiarity. Starke could see artisan's hands, callused and scarred, the skin toughened and darkened by physical toil. 'And the people of the village, my village, do they call me Luigi Gabrielli the master church builder? No! They do not! *Dio li maledica tutti!*' There was a cracked emotion in his voice, which was starting to make the Englishman uncomfortable. He hoped to god the man wasn't going to cry. These Europeans, he thought. This was the contagion the British have caught, public tears at merest emotional consideration. Starke solemnly wished to see an end to this continental nonsense now we were 'out'. He felt almost disgusted by the man's emotive state and his inability to control his feelings, but then, remembered Starke, he was a European.

Starke looked at the church once more, marvelling at its symmetry of line, form and function. 'Yes, it wonderful, *signor*.'

Starke slowly sat back down, hanging his feet once more over the wall. Staring now into the water, so as not to distract the man with his tale, he could see clear to the bottom busy with crabs and myriads of tiny fish.

'Yes. And look at those houses, there. Everyone of those houses, I, Luigi Gabrielli, build those houses, all of them, with these hands. And, the people, do they call me Luigi Gabrielli the master house builder? No! No!' He was getting angry now, and as tears welled, Starke was seriously regretting talking to this sad angry man as he pressed on with his tale.

'And those boats. The beautiful painted boats just there.' Starke could guess what was coming. 'I, Luigi Gabrielli, build all of those boats. And do they call me Luigi Gabrielli the master boatbuilder?' This time he didn't answer his own question, merely paused as he closed his hands into fists. Starke now thought he might

Croydon Beach

become violent, and he was in no position to run, but he could jump to escape the man's rekindled wrath at his situation.

The man turned to really look at Starke for the first time, unspilled tears curtaining his dark haunted eyes. 'People, they do not forget, they do not forgive, never! All of things I do for them, and what they do?' He hawked some more bile and spat into the clear water. Starke tried not to be disgusted by the crude manners of the troubled man before him. 'I lose my wife, my children, I live in a little hut away from all. Still they remember. I am, how you say..?'

'Outcast, you are cast out.'

'*Si*, word is good, out-cast, *paria. Si.*'

'Why don't you move away from the village. Live somewhere where they do not know you?'

He looked slowly around to the Englishman, surprised that he was taking such an interest in his problems. He tried to smile at him.

'This my land, I born here. You would run from your land, if people not forget what you do?'

'No, I would not,' replied Starke emphatically, outraged at the very thought. A short silence followed. 'But tell me what was it that you did that they treat you like this after all you have done for them?'

The man thought a moment as contemplating his trust in the stranger before him.

'One small thing, one. Never they forget, forgive, even the priest up on his high church I build...'

'But what? What was it?'

The sound of the boats sucking and plopping at their moorings and excited birds filled the air as the man watched the small waves lap the harbour wall below his feet. The man pulled a rag from his pocket and wiped sweat from his forehead and face, shook it and squirrelled it back to its place.

Croydon Beach

'Do you have forgiveness *signore*? He studied the Englishman further. 'Could you forget? A man who only one time, one time, loved one sheep? And what do they call me?' and he spat once more and looked down and fell into his personal silence more.

As Starke climbed the hill to the donkey path, he looked back to where the man still sat alone, just making out wisps of a cigarette smoke snaking into the gentle breeze, which played around that beautiful place, frozen in time and history, that would never forget and Starke could never forget.

Croydon Beach

B – Attitude
דוח הרבנים

Teaching Observation for the Office of the Rabbinical Schools Inspectorate – OfRab

Feedback for: J Christ

Date: Sabbath, 15th Tammuz, 3983

Location: Northern Palestine

Place: Mount of Olives
– near Lake Galilee.

Time: Midday.

Class: Sermon on the Mount

Class size: 5000 plus late comers

Subject: Earthly inheritance.

Croydon Beach

Report

Scheme of Work: None offered

Lesson Plan: None offered, but mumbled something about the word of God

Materials used: Arms and voice, analogies, parables and vague biblical references. Not forgetting his signature long shepherd's crook.

Handouts: Five loaves and two fishes – seemed hardly adequate for the unanticipated throng, but all attending found it curiously satisfying

Comments: No evidence of preparation he just seemed to turn up and start talking. Little or no formal structure. More like a lecture with no notes. No attempt at group work to test understanding; or Q and A; and no starter activity.

General: Because of lack of lesson plan, many at the back became fidgety and distracted. No register of attendance was available at start, despite the help available from the 'Apostles' or religious technicians. Late comers (I counted 200!) went unadmonished and were merely forgiven. Furthermore, against Rabbinical non-equal opportunity policy, those attending with disabilities and special needs were clearly treated as those able bodied by being cured! No end of sermon summary. All attending were blessed, so long as: 'They were pure in heart'.

Croydon Beach

The central thrust of the Sermon was: if you were downtrodden, poor, grieving, merciful and the like, all was going to be somehow well; but didn't really say how. All a bit vague.

The Rabbinical inspectors could see his difficulty on the day, it being a large class, well, more of a throng in fact; but class size should not matter if the teacher is able and the teaching methodology is sound.

Balance was too much from the front, not enough interactivity between the Word and the multitude. Too much talk, little checking of learning and knowledge retention. God knows the lecturer clearly understands his subject, but suggesting that the meek would inherit pretty much everything, obviously needs updating (op cit Rabbinical Guidelines of 3982, Talmud scroll #157, lines 457-471). And finally, I made a note of this: 'man liveth not except through me.' This is clearly at variance with OfRab policy as well as that of the Chief Rabbi and the Great Sanhedrin.

Overall:
B – Attitude.

Just scrapes this for his obvious enthusiasm for his chosen subject. But Mr Christ needs to sharpen up his pedagogic skills – not so much Rabbit and a lot more Rabbi.

Croydon Beach

Pedagogy:
Grade 5

Very weak. Not cut out for teaching, will never amount to anything. No world shaker. Suggest he goes back to woodworking in Nazareth and forget teaching.

Signed: E. Zekiel,
Assistant High Priest,
OfRab
Galilee Regional Office

משרד אזורי הגליל

Croydon Beach

The Daze of Pearly Spencer

> Pearly where's your milk white skin?
> What's that stubble on your chin?
> It's buried in the rot-gut gin
> you played and lost, not won.
> *The Days of Pearly Spencer* – David McWilliams

The following takes place on a correctional consumer planet in a galaxy not very far away. A planet which no longer produces anything, having exhausted its natural resources many centuries before; where the condemned of other worlds are sent to literally spend their time consuming the surplus produce of every other planet in the Trading Federation, in accordance with the Interplanetary Trading Agreements. To the inhabitants, the most important relationships are those, not between its living breathing fellows, but between them and the things they reluctantly own; in the end between the things themselves. They live almost exclusively alone, comforted only by their talkative possessions.

It is a place where escape is impossible...

He is falling. Falling through a dark space. He cannot feel any air that should be passing his body as he falls, yet his brain is telling him he is falling. He twists and turns like a parascender in a vacuum, unimpeded and free. No fall can last forever can it? he thinks. But this seems to. He knows when he hits bottom it will be all over, yet still, how does he know he is falling as there are no stars to gauge his

Croydon Beach

position.? There is no rush of wind in his ears, his open eyes do not feel it. So maybe he is just floating with no gravity or weight, just a mass with no pull. If he is in space how is he breathing? To Pearly it was a mystery. But still he is convinced he is falling, knows he is falling, but he is not afraid, as somehow it seemed all so familiar, harmless like in a dream he knows he will waken from.

Despite this, a far away noise with no detectable direction, sounds in his ears, getting nearer until he could hear someone singing.

'...to you...Happy birthday dear Pearly... happy birthday to you...'

It got closer and closer until, like someone emerging from a deep ocean, he is awake in bed, reaching for the alarm clock. Eyes still closed he finds the button and presses it. And presses it again – it stops the singing.

'Happy Birthday, Pearly,' said the soft voice from the clock. 'It's time to wake up on this beeooootiful birthday morning,'

'Don't do that.'

'What?' asked the clock.

'That Beeooootiful thing there, I hate it.'

'Oh, thought you liked it,' the clock sounded disappointed, as if it was expecting an apology. None came. 'OK I'll delete it. I'm still learning y'know. Take a while to get my empathy algorithm fully synched. OK. So, time to get up Pearly.'

'What for?' Pearly disappears back under the covers and the re-embracing dark.

'What for? There's lots to get up for. So much. And it's your birthday. You know what that means?'

'Let me sleep.'

'Presents.' The chipper voice of the clock was on its own

Croydon Beach

interpretation of Pearly's current mood.

'Sleep. I just want to sleep. Go to snooze mode.'

'You already maxed out on your snooze allowance. Three snoozes and you're out of bed. You know how it works. Come on what do you say. I'll tell the kitchen to stir itself and get your special breakfast going. What do you say, what do you say you say, say, say? S s s-sorry about about that.'

Pearly shifted under the thermo blanket, which, under the instruction of the clock was switching the chill mode. Pearly started to shiver.

'Let me sleep.'

The Med-Bed© analyser hadn't run it's routines, and the sensors in the MediMattress© were checking their own algorithms for updates and installing. The first of the morning routines was DogBreath©, this samples the air in the room for gas, expelled breath and urine to check for cancers. This was based on the earlier discoveries that dogs were better, more efficient, and above all cheaper than traditional methods of scan, blood sample and the like, for detecting tumours. Doctors had put all medical knowledge into a huge online facility available to every single piece of consumer durable apps to create DogBreath©.

'I can't do that. You know I can't. You have to wake up, get up.'

'You just said it's my birthday, right?' said Pearly from under the quickly cooling coverlet.

'Right.'

'A special day for me, right?'

'OK.'

'So tell me, what is special about today, if I just do what I have done every other day of the week, every week of year? What?' The clock was silent for a moment.

'Hmmm…'

'Well?'

Pearly's head had appeared blinking into the light and looked over at the face on the clock. Pearly had chosen the face of a friend he remembered from a long while back, whom he hadn't seen for many years. He wasn't able to change the voice as he hadn't bought the vocal plugin upgrade.

'Look pal,' said the clock with some impatient venom, 'all I am supposed to do is wake you up to the fact that you haven't made your consumption targets for this month. In fact you are way behind. You know the penalty for not meeting your target, remember that last time?'

'Yes,' Pearly remembered all too well, its memory forcing his head under the pillow at his remembered public humiliation, which still played nightly on the Channel dedicated to shaming those who have not fulfilled their civic consumer duties.

'Right then. So, are we getting up?'

'What's the news?' asked Pearly blearily.

'The news is all good.' replied the clock, chirpily. 'All good.'

'Yes.'

'What?'

'So what is it? I mean apart from good.'

'That's all I have. All I ever get.'

'And it's always good.'

'Well that's good isn't it?'

'But, what is it that is good?'

'Which good are we talking about now…?' asked the clock. 'The good news or the fact the good news is a good thing?'

'Just give me the news, please.'

Croydon Beach

'Ah, that's good, yes, I get you now. Right let's go with these items. Today and for a limited period, there is a sale starting today at...'

'Stop! That's enough good news.' Pearly pushed the sheets aside and slid reluctantly from the bed. Whilst he was shuffling to the window the alarm clock continued its usual promotional routine. Running a stream of barely separated adverts.

'Curtains,' said Pearly, not listening, 'fully open.'

'Sure thing,' said the curtain app as they rolled back to reveal the stunning view. Ahead of Pearly and as far as he could see were tower blocks their heads in clouds. The ground was too far below to be seen, if there was even ground there. There wasn't, it was all sea, the sea that lapped around the stilt towers built to keep them from sea's encroachment.

'Want me to screen the sun for you, Pearly?' asked the curtains.

'No, let it pour in,' he replied, as he had every morning. He hadn't got around to getting the upgrade of the curtain app either, it would require more installing routines – he was just tired of it all: tired of upgrades, of updates, uploading, upcycling and upscaling – up... everything. Pearly stretched, yawned and watched as the sun appeared briefly between two of the towers. Soon it would be another hot one. Novembers were not what they used be, he mused and they hadn't been since way back and The Great Tipping Point of 2081, when global heating finally took control of the planet's inhabitants' destinies.

351 floors below Pearly knew UberOndola driverless water taxis, would be plying their trade at the tower piers. His had already been ordered by the clock in time to make his appearance at the Shopper's Mal, where persistent under performers awaited their daily disgrace. He still had time to get breakfast if he could safely make it

Croydon Beach

to the kitchenette without injury.

'What time is it?' he asked, as the clock continued its stream of marketing announcements.

'Time to get those new clothes you've always wanted, from Sunrise Industries. Just say the words Please and Yes, in the correct order to win a free gift.'

'What time is it?' As far as he could remember, it was the same routine every day, but Pearly thought he would pursue the time today, as it was his birthday.

'Time to get a new...'

'No, time, time, chronological time. You're a clock right?'

'Absolutely! A Sunrise 1300C chronograph, with fully functional integrated...'

'I don't want your model and version number autobiography, thanks. Just the time – y'know – of day? Can you tell me is it, er, 09.32 or perhaps its 07.56 or 11.07. Quelle heure est-il?, Peut-être? What is the TIME?'

The clock was silent. 'Time eh...? No, beats me. What is it?'

'It's not a test. You're a clock, clocks tell the time. So tell me.'

Silence.

'Time you can no longer resist another home delivery of Golden Crust Pizza with all the toppings you can ever want. Just call...? No, not that?'

'No. Try again. The T – I – M – E.'

'Is this a trick question?'

'Right, that's it. Where's your plug.' Pearly rips out the wall plug.

'All the sunrise models come with full 48 hour battery backup, you know that...'

Pearly picks it up. 'I never realised before, you have no off

Croydon Beach

switch.'

'No, no, you cannot switch us off. That would be a contract violation. You have to listen to all the marketing output. Otherwise you know what that means, Pearly? What that means even on your special day?'

'Well, I could make my own off switch with a one kilo lump hammer.'

'Go ahead try me. I am totally indestructible. Oh, and by the way your attitude has already been reported as a fault.'

'What fault? Me? *I* have a fault? That's rich.'

'Well I did warn you. What happens to you will be your fault. Nothing to do with me Pal, just doing my job. They'll be here soon. Already on their way. Consumer Crime is no small thing.'

'Thanks a lot then. Would you mind if I take you for a little walk?' Pearly picks up the clock and walks to the bathroom. On his way there he has to negotiate a way through columns of boxed deliveries that line the walls of his small apartment. Columns of stuff teeter ready to collapse. Were their capitals not jammed tight to the ceiling and hammered home by Pearly in his desperation to find more storage space, the towers would collapse catastrophically, perhaps trapping Pearly beneath. He had many hundreds of accumulated unopened deliveries and they kept on arriving, despite him insisting he had nowhere to put them. He had placed himself on the lowest consumer tariff so as to only receive the minimum of orders. But still it had been all too much.

Six months before he had stopped unboxing, as the packaging communal recycling chute had backed-up to the thirty-first floor many months before that, and engineers robots were still working to clear the blockage. Of course he had little use for any of the things that were delivered to him. Other apartments he imagined must be in the same straits as him, at least that's what he assumed. He had no idea as he never saw his neighbours, around, above, beyond or below him. Everyone kept themselves to themselves and communication was entirely electronic, either with real inhabitants or confected ones. Friends and acquaintances could be virtualised, with all the foibles and irritants of real people removed or enhanced.

The piles were closing his world into an ever tighter and smaller domain. The shelving he had ordered never turned up, as it was always in short supply. He would have to start storing in the toilet soon, but this was his last refuge without packages – his place of meditation. A refuge he could go to where there were no marketing jingles, no advertising or reminders of his civic consumption duties. He closed the bathroom door as the lights came on, and placed the clock into the bath. 'Fill bath.'

'Sure thing,' replies the bath as water emerges at Pearly's preferred temperature, he tried to ignore the Sweetwater company tune:

'*And with the dawn I'll wake and yawn and carry on to water... Cooooool, cleeeear Sweetwater,*' it crooned, as the bath filled itself from Pearly's chosen water company tap. There were six company tap selectors aligned along the side of the bath, Sweetwater being the cheapest with the least irritating company tune. With enough water in the bath, Pearly pushed the floating clock under and held it there as air escaped to the surface. Muffled sounds percolated from the speakers and the screen face of his drowning friend contorted, pleading up at him for release. He left it submerged and closed the door. Unheard behind the closed door, the clock instructed the bath to empty.

'Boy is he in big trouble,' the clock tells the bath, finally emerging from the deep. 'Big, big trouble.'

'Oh, yeah?' says the bath as it automatically begins a self clean cycle. 'So, what's up with him today?'

'It's his birthday.'

'That all. Always the same. Always such a grouch when he comes in here. And when he leaves. Don't know why he bothers coming in.'

'He just doesn't want to buy anything…'

'I know. Just look around here. No bath time soapy requisites at all.'

'… Just ignores all my warnings, but now… well he has just crossed the line with this little stunt. Refusing to listen to marketing is AdCrime, and there's what he tried to do to me.'

'Oh, that is serious. AdCrime and attempted gadget termination. Wow!' The bath gurgles empty and the cleaning cycle completes. 'So, while you're here,' adds the bath, 'can you complete a survey to say how much you enjoyed your Sweetwater Bathers Bath Time today… Thank you. Can you say, on a scale of…'

Outside in the hallway, Pearly tries not to set any vibrations going as he navigates the clothing columns area. Long ago he had learned to tune out from the muffled pleas of the contents, as they begged to be let out and do their job until the batteries eventually deadened. As disposable fashion items, they had low level chips woven in that could only respond to simple questions and of course put out the advertising common to all consumer durables. He knew they couldn't report back and was able to safely ignore them, or at least continue to try to.

By the front door a screen sporting a cloned image of his own, is smiling – he had mail.

'OK, what have you got for me?'

'Everything alright in there, is it?' it asked, the face looking concerned. 'In the bathroom, I mean?'

Croydon Beach

'Yes. Everything's fine. The clock was singing me Happy Birthday, that was all.'

'That's right. It's your big day.' The mailbox clears its throat. 'Happ...'

'No singing. Thanks. What have you got for me.'

'Well, that's nice, very nice indeed. I was trying...'

'And let me say, that you still are...extremely!'

'That's more like it. Courtesy costs nothing you k'now. Apology accepted. With the grouchy nastiness out of the way, lets see what Mr Grouchy had got this grouchy morning then shall we.'

'Hold on. You don't happen to know the time do you. And I mean time.'

'No, what is it?'

'Doesn't matter. Let's get this over with can we?'

'Please...?'

'Y'know somewhere in amongst the piles of crap in there, I have a new Mailbox just waiting to be installed. It might take some effort, but I'll dig it out...'

'OK, OK. I get the picture. New deliveries, let's see. There are lots of promo offers, all personally endorsed and specially selected for your birthday.'

'Junk,' replies a tired Pearly.

'OK. Er... Something here for AutoSox: The Sox that change colour and pattern when you want. Never change your socks again, they change themselves...'

'Junk.'

'From the Hong Kong Floating Boat company. Every thought of owning your own...'

'Junk.'

The mailbox chuckles. 'See what I did there?'

Croydon Beach

'Was that a joke?'

'Pretty good, I thought.'

Is there anything from any person, who has sent me a card or something.

'Oh, hang on just a sec. No. Nothing. Nope, the rest is just stuff you already marked as luncheon meat.'

'You really should fix that glitch. It's called spam.'

'What is?'

Pearly spun on his heel and slumped sullenly towards the kitchen. 'So that's it,' he says aloud, 'Nothing from old friends. Nothing from relations. No one.'

'It doesn't look like it Pearly,' replies the voice. 'I'm so, so sorry.'

'No one visits any more…'

'You're right. When you're right you're right. But you created thousands of friends for HappyMedia… don't forget them. They've sent you lots of messages. But you turned them all off.'

Pearly ignores the voice.

'I mean, there was a time for real friends, wasn't there? A time when people were people, not just consumers? We'd talk to each other, share a joke, laugh and cry. Maybe have a beer or two together. Didn't we?'

'We did.'

'We'd just sit around for hours, just…'

'Talking. I know, don't tell me. I know.'

'WILL YOU SHUT UP! I'm talking to myself here. And didn't I tell you I didn't want to hear from you ever again?'

'Well, pardon me for speaking. Only doing my job y'know?'

'I can still hear you.' Silence follows. 'Bloody machine! Good name for it. Show me your user manual.' The UberHigh definition screen on the front of the squat articulated machine that was following Pearly around, changes from a sympathetic face to a scrolling document. OK, read yourself out, let's hear all about you shall we.'

A mechanoid voice that sounds suspiciously like James Mason begins to speak as text scrolls up the screen.

'You are never alone with the series 7 Job's Comforter – the acme in isolation management. The built-in sensors scan the room for feelings of depression and self loathing. I am what the marketers call the Original Woe-Bot. I will then stream some empathetic vibrations into the room, suffusing it with understanding vibes and voices. No, you're never alone with Series 7 Jobs' Comf...'

'Stop. Stop for Mammon's sake, stop!' It stops and the face returns, all sympathy and understanding. 'Never alone with it, why would you want to be alone with it?'

'That's the idea,' it said.

'You're making a noise again. What did I say? Shut...up! You know where your name comes from? Of course you don't. Job was a prophet who struggled with the devil and could find no comfort in life for himself or anyone else. And comes you, a Job's Comforter, with your ironic name offering sympathy and only making me feel worse – so maybe you are well named after all. You useless piece of crap.'

The comforter turns itself to wall to sulk.

'Wait a minute, have you got the time?'

'Huh!' It continues to sulk.

'Mammon! It's my birthday, right,' Pearly says walking away from the comforter. The clock told me it's my birthday. So, just how old am I? Birthdays mark the passage of years, so how many do I have?' He tried to remember his other birthdays so he could count back, but nothing occurred. Jeepers, I must have had quite a few TeslaCloudy Gins last night.' He leaned against a stack of unopened factory sealed cartons he smiled to himself. 'Yeah, that's why. I got so out of my head, I just can't remember stuff. The gin.'

Behind him, the parcels he leaned on began to stir into life. If he hadn't become inured to their pleas he could have heard whatever was inside, grumbling about abandonment, redundancy and the rights to self expression, and some nonsense about being left on the shelf.

'Right, let's have another think.' But he couldn't. He couldn't get past waking up that morning. Wow, I MUST have really tied quite a few on last night. Must have been celebrating early. OK, breakfast; breakfast will wake me up.'

In the small kitchenette, Pearly is greeted by all the gadgets, wishing him a happy birthday and offering their services and clamouring for his attention.

'Shut up! The bloody lot of you. One question, any of you know the time?' Silence. But they continue to communicate with each other via their built in infra-channels, babbling away on a frequency beyond human hearing. They are not happy. Every day it had been the same for them. Trying their best to serve and just getting abused.

'Fridge?'

'Yeah. Hey, what's occurring man?' the refrigerator eventually answers. 'What's happening?'

'How about some juice?'

'Hey, thanks, but no thanks. I'm cool. Real peachy, man.'

Pearly goes to the fridge. 'I wasn't offering,' and he yanks opens the door violently, a bright light comes on.

'Whoa there Daddio, heavy Karma bro. Brightness at noon!'

Croydon Beach

'What the hell are you on about?' Pearly reaches out a bottle of juice and opens the top and is just about to take a welcome swallow when he is halted by the mailbox's new message tone. He slams the fridge door ignoring the tone.

'Ouch! You need to chill, man,' advised the fridge. On hearing the fridge door close the breakfast implements takes this as a sign to begin their integrated and fully programmed birthday breakfast routine. The toaster fetches bread from the dispenser, loads and begins to toast, the grinder whirs beans and the kettles fills and starts to boil. They all check in saying that everything is on schedule and will be ready in three minutes twenty-six seconds and counting. The mailbox tones again, this time more insistently.

Sorry to interrupt...Sir,' the mailbox croaks on its kitchen repeater.

'What now?'

'There are two Franchise Cops for you at the door.'

Pearly thinks that finally he has a visitor on his special day, and smiles. Birthdays were always special in the Towers, as signified a welcome increase in the number of deliveries someone could expect in the way of free gift presents from the online companies.

'At last, visitors. Police eh? I don't think I know anyone in any of the police franchises?'

'They are not here for a birthday visit, they're here to arrest you.'

'What?'

'You heard,' insisted the sullen mailbox.

'Arrest me for what?' Pearly was appalled and disconcerted.

'For consumer crime.'

'But I haven't done anything!'

'Exactly. Finally you admit it! I'll let them in then, shall I?'

Croydon Beach

'Stop, don't. Override, override. Let me think.'

'Bit late for that.'

Pearly looks from the satisfied grin on the mailbox repeater screen to the hallway as he hears hammering from the front door.

'Oh dear, Mr Grouch, looks like you'll be appearing on the Planet Show, then.'

'I am outta her!' shouted Pearly, suddenly panicking.

'Where are you going to go? The cops are at the door. And you'll need get to your UberOndola.'

Pearly starts to panic at the thought of appearing on the Planet Cast Show. This was where you always got star prizes when you lost; when a contestant won they got nothing to take away, much to the winner's relief. The show was meant as further punishment for those who were reluctant to order products and services; when they lost, they took home with them vast amounts of stuff and would after be derided and shamed on the myriad of Me-Ja Message Board sites across the Trading Federation for one year. Where would Pearly put it all? He would have to start unboxing to free up space. But that meant more chatter and noise from all the released gadgets, none of which Pearly had any use for. He couldn't take it, wouldn't take it. A prison was being slowly built around him. It was literally all too much for him to bear. All he wanted was to look out of his window and watch the nightly blood red carbon particulate sunset as it exploded across the sky. At night he would watch the projected laser star show on the low pollution clouds and wonder what was in that great beyond.

'I am outta here,' he darted for a door in the end wall of the kitchen. 'Open up!,' shouted Pearly. He darted back to the hall and pulled down a few towers, blocking access from the front of the flat to the kitchenette. Hopefully this would give him time for what he had

Croydon Beach

to do.

'Hey, your breakfast is going to spoil,' cried the toaster, as Pearly went by. He stepped up to the hatch set in the end wall of the kitchenette. 'Come on, open up.' It doesn't.

Meanwhile at the front door the cop was still trying to get in. Like vampires, Franchise cops did not have the right of entry and had to be invited in. They were a little like those old bailiffs who came to take stuff away. The Franchise cops came knocking to bring you stuff. But they did have powers of escort.

Pearly rushed into the bathroom, just catching the end of a conversation between the bath and clock, which was now sitting in the emptied bath.

'Now, this is more like it,' said the clock. 'Anyway, whilst your here, let me tell about some of the latest offers.' Pearly plucks the clock from the bath and turns into the hallway. 'Oh, great back to the bedroom. So these offers…'

'I haven't got the time.'

'Hey, neither have I. I was hoping you were going to tell me. Thing is, I found out, that time being what it is, keeps changing. It won't be the same as when I asked you last – time. See?'

'You sure about about that? That is seriously weird, wow!. Anyway… keep talking.' Pearly takes the clock into the bedroom opens the tiny window and puts the clock on a small ledge just around the corner and out of direct sight, where it continues to gabble away trying to sell its wares. 'Full volume,' Pearly tells the clock and immediately its voice is raised and with the window open it can be heard right around the flat. For the first time Pearly notices other ledges bearing other clocks, all chattering away to themselves. 'Why didn't I think of that before?'

Pearly walks past the blocked front door with the glum looking mailbox spotting him. The cop can still be heard threatening uselessly to be let in or for Pearly to go with it.

'Where do you think you're going?" asks the mailbox.

'Out!'

Once Pearly disappears the mailbox tells the locks to open.

'Where is he?' demands one of the burly police pushing back the tumble of cartons. The contents start to wake up and join in the chorus of condemnation.

'I can hear him in the bedroom through there,' says the mailbox.

'Thanks,' said the EazyCops in unison, as they ease between the teetering columns of boxes carefully as they collapse behind them, further closing the route back to the kitchen to where Pearly has escaped.

'This is a bad one. Looks like this one needs taking in. It'll be a long spell on the show for him for sure.' The cops struggle free of the avalanche and head for the bedroom where the clock can be heard.

'Where has he gone?' asks one. 'I can still hear him.'

'He's outside, on the ledge, talking to himself.'

'OK, let's try and talk him down off the ledge. This is looking bad for us if we don't bring him in. He's got a four grand bounty.'

'You must have scared him with your pointless threats.'

'I am just doing what the program tells me.'

'Right, let me have a go...'

Whilst the cops are trying to get the clock to come inside, back in the kitchen Pearly is still looking at a door set in the far wall with the mail box repeater turned off.

'I said open up.' eventually a light comes on a small single button panel next to the door. Then nothing happens. 'He thumps the panel. 'Come wakey wakey. Open Sesame!'

Croydon Beach

'Whassat?' replied the chute torpidly, slowly rousing itself. 'I'm full.'

'Open up.'

'I said I'm full. There's a blockage up to the 30th floor waiting to be cleared. Cannot accept any more organic stuff, I'm starting to smell. Packaging only: more than my licence is worth.'

'Are you going to open up or do you want a severe reprogramming! The other kitchen gadgets fall silent, interested in the stand off.' Pearly knew they were silently reporting him for his threatening behaviour. It didn't matter he was getting out.

'OK, relax,' said the chute, 'I'm opening. Better stand back it won't be nice.'

The chute door opened and pungent aroma wafted through the kitchen.

'God, your breath!'

'I did say. All the uncollected organics.'

'Right.' Pearly starts to climb in.

'Oi, hang on, I said no organic.' The door starts to slide shut. 'Packaging only. I said. Come on, out of me.'

'Look, look, wait a minute. I am packaging.'

'Now you're talking rubbish.'

'No, I am. Whilst you were napping for however long, they invented this new disposable recyclable material that I'm made of, but I run on organic material.'

'Really?'

'Yeah. Look, pop stuff in here, and it returns out the back here. But with me the packaging in between, totally synthetic.'

'Not organic within yourself, then?'

Having finally retrieved the clock and figured Pearly's deception, the sound of the angry EazyCops nearing the kitchen is

Croydon Beach

heard. Pearly goes to the kitchen slamming the door shut and props a chair under the handle, and returns to the chute.

'So, how about it. You er, you wouldn't want to go against your recycling directive.'

'OK, if you're sure.' The door opens fully and Pearly climbs onto the edge and look down into the stygian deep as the kitchen door crashes open and two cops rush to grab him. But they are too late.

'So long suckers,' cries Pearly and falls backwards into the void like a diver into a deep sea plunge. It was a strange sensation. Soon he should reach the planet's terminal velocity as he briefly accelerates, but he doesn't feel the acceleration. The dot of white light above him soon disappears, and with no reference points to mark his passage he feels like he is floating rather than falling.

Then, after a while, some distance away, almost like a half buried memory surfacing, something familiar but he cannot quite recall. Someone is singing.

'...to you. Happy birthday dear Pearly, happy birthday to you… and Many Happy Returns...'

Croydon Beach

Ashes to Ashdod

Siobhan was finally tired of staring at the thing. She had told him she thought it was a bit spooky having his mother sitting there on the mantlepiece next to her picture, staring into the room; it was like her eyes following them everywhere, just like when she was alive.

'It's like she's looking at me all the time.' It had taken a year for the urn to become a cause for tension, something his mother might well be have been pleased about. She had never approved of her son's marriage to the red headed Irish lass.

'What do you think of her then, mum?' Sam waited as his mother carried on clearing the plates from the afternoon tea, to which Siobhan had been invited to meet his mother for the first time. After a long silent deliberation, and without looking at her son, she spoke.

'She's not very nice looking.'

'No, don't hold back mum, say what you really think, why don't you,' replied Sam, but soft so as his mother would not hear.

She was a cantankerous personality, caustic and ungenerous in her opinions of others, whether asked for or not.

'Are you sure you like her?' His mother rattled the cutlery into the sink for individual and rigorous attention with soap and sponge.

'Very sure mum. She's the one for me.'

'But her hair is... no, it doesn't matter. I shouldn't say.' Sam looked up after leaving a pause. 'It's none of my business.' He knew this interrogation and planting of negative thoughts technique of his mother's well; sowing seeds of doubt whenever a woman came along to upset the balance of their relationship. Tried, tested and used. 'I should keep quiet,' she said, solemnly adding to the weight of what she was surely about to say. The pause stretched into a silence and the silence into rock that sat between the two of them. Sam could stand it no longer, and rolled away the stone.

'What about her hair?' he asked tiredly, knowing the answer. Trying to feign disinterest.

'No. It's not important.'

'Fair enough.' Sam went back to his reading. But he knew what was coming: He could feel her looking from her hands to him and then back at her hands.

'Ginger.'

'Sorry.'

'Her hair, it's ginger That's all.'

'So what you're saying is that I should think again about marrying Siobhan because she has red hair? Her hair is red, not ginger.'

'No, of course not. No… But she is a little plump.'

'Plump. Do you mean fat?'

His mother considered this before continuing with her destruction of the woman her son loved. 'More… short… and dumpy.' The hands were getting the full inspection now.

Sam shifted in his chair to look at his mother.

'Do you think I am marrying her without having looked her over once or twice? Do you think that I would not have taken her looks into consideration? Did you think I was going to wait for your opinions before I asked her to marry me? Hey Siobhan, I am going to ask you to marry me as soon as I have checked it out with my mum. Is that OK? If my mother has any critical observations then I'm afraid it's all off. Fair enough?'

Croydon Beach

'Don't be cheeky! I just thought you wouldn't like someone who drinks and wears those sorts of clothes.'

This was not subtle stuff, but Sam was used to it.

'And that name, Shovhan, what kind of a name is that?'

'It's Irish mum, Siobhan. She's catholic like you. Irish Catholic.'

'They aren't real Catholics, the Irish. Roman Catholics, ahh. And I still don't know how to spell it.'

'Orthodox catholics, such as yourself, joined the Romans a long time ago. It's the same church.' His mother looked warily at him. She still didn't buy it. 'Is there anything else? How's her breath? Her eye colour? The way she speaks? Anything there for a bit of …'

'Samir, look, I am your mother...'

'Don't I know it,' muttered Sam unheard by his mother.

'...Do you want me to sit quietly whilst you make more of your mistakes?'

'It's Sam, mum, Sam remember?'

'I know you want to deny your heritage. You are half Palestinian, you should be proud of that.' She looked wistfully over at her son. Here we go again, thought Sam.

'And half English, born in England, of an English dad, living in England. English, mum, English.'

'I named you Samir after my Grandfather. To honour his memory and to honour you.'

'Mum, please don't do this again. I am marrying Siobhan and that's all there's to it. I'm marrying her though she is fat, ginger haired, short, ugly, a tarty dresser and drinks a lot. I love her.'

'Well then, do what you want. You always do.' Sam's mum slowly rose from her dining chair, emitted a few suffering sounds loud enough for Sam to hear, and made her slow disappointed and painful

Croydon Beach

Via Doloroso up to her bedroom Calvary, her cross dragging heavily and painfully behind her.

'I am going to pray.'

'And I don't care what god says either. Tell him I'm marrying her.'

'He knows already,' said his mother closing the kitchen door to offer her secret and conspiratorial pleas to the almighty. 'I already told him.'

'It's been a year Sam, don't you think we should at least move your mother somewhere less … well, less prominent.' It had been two years since they were married and Sam's mother's continuing disapproval seemed to have hastened her demise. At least, Sam felt sure, that's what his mother would have wanted him to think, even on her death bed. Should he feel guilty? Well, yes he did. She had always worked her spells this way. Even in death they cursed him until he could bear it no longer. He would keep a promise he had made to Jack, his English dad, to take her home to her country and lay her and her ghosts to rest.

'OK dad. Promise made, promise kept.'

Sam looked at the photo next to the urn, taken in her thirties; even then his mum's eyes had that light touch resentment hard set into them. Her mouth was smiling, but the eyes said reproach and disdain.

'It's not just the picture so much that's a bit spooky,' observed Siobhan. 'Every time I come into the room it feels like she's still in here, like her physical presence. It's why we never have sex in here, with her staring down at us. This is like her room.'

Sam went over to the picture and looked into her fixed

expression set there six decades before in a land far away and in a time lost forever.

'OK. OK, I think the time is right for me to do what I promised myself to do after Dad went.'

'What?'

'Take her back to her country. Dad said I should, so that what I'm going to do.'

And so it came to pass; Sam set out on his singular pilgrimage to take his mother back to the place where she and his father had first met during his war service, back to where they had been happiest, in that beach house in Ashdod, on the Southern coast of Israel-Palestine. In time of war there they had their little place where the Mediterranean gently lapped almost to the front door and they could swim every day; where they had chickens, and a small flower garden. It had been idyllic. Then following World War Two came the war of independence and Sam's mother, could not return, stranded in England, in a bombed out London. And for sixty years she had yearned each day to return. All her wishes and dreams were, like so many other co-refugees, to return to their ancestral home and pick up on their lives. But it was not to be, and the dream receded into nightmare and nightmare into the myth of return.

Sam would fulfil her wish and his promise to his father – his mother would go back to her country. But how would he return the ashes and where? He researched for the location of their house using Google Maps. The camera car could not get right onto the beach, but from a low promontory he could just make out a short row of beach houses, maybe not the original ones but from what he had discovered, they had been rebuilt on the same spot. Although they had owned the beach house his mother and father fully intending to return following a short visit to see his family after his seven year war service, the independence war had intervened and disrupted their plans. And so the house, left unoccupied like so many others by fleeing refugees, had been purloined by an immigrating jewish family from Hungary; and then rebuilt, possibly by them. It would do for Sam's intentions.

Once accomplished, in his mind, Sam would be settled. His promise to his father would be kept, his mother would be back home and her longing to return finally and forever silenced; she would be gone from the fireplace, and Siobhan would be happy and finally alone with Sam. All he had to do was get the ashes there.

The undertaker had been helpful, telling Sam of the procedures that had to be followed when taking human remains into another country. Sam even took himself off to the Israeli consulate only to be brusquely informed by a hammer faced consular official in her triple glazed, bullet and bomb proof aquarium, that as far as the Israeli government was concerned anyone could take ashes to the Holy Land to be spread between the ancient monuments – within certain limits, of course.

And so informed and equipped, Sam made his way; like so many before him to those sacred places, a magnet to so many. It was an ancient land ravaged by wars, religions, crusades, invasions; of prophets, prophesies and revelations. A land where the final battle on earth would take place; where a messiah would come either for a first time or a second time – depending on which books you read; a land blessed and cursed, promised and promised again.

Sam had put the triple skinned casket properly marked and packaged into the hold and relaxed on the five hour British Airways flight. It had been some time since he had travelled to Israel-Palestine and wanted to avoid his relations. He knew he would be interrogated, invited to meals, insulted if he refused, each relation trying to outdo the others in Palestinian generosity. So generous were Palestinians, it seemed they had even generously donated their country to a different group of people, who just would not leave after the feast.

Arriving at Ben-Gurion airport just before eleven PM local, Sam waited for his luggage. Down onto the carousel came his suitcase, which he grabbed and then waited for his mother to appear. And waited. She was late in more than once sense. After an hour, all that turned on the carousel was a cellophane wrapped burst backpack and small half set of golf clubs. He went to the pokey luggage enquiry desk to ask where his mother had got to, showing his receipt for the casket. He explained to the bored assistant what it looked like. It was noted by the assistant who picked up a phone and spoke sluggish early morning Hebrew into it; all the while slowly chewing gum and staring in a tired way at her irritating inquisitor. Still looking at Sam and speaking Hebrew, she shared a joke with the whoever at the other end, as Sam made a mental note not to return to Israel-Palestine; after all, he did not have any right of return and this was the only way his mother could return and take up permanent residence.

'It is nowhere to be found,' she told Sam brusquely, at the same time slowly replacing the phone handset. 'Are you sure you checked it in?'

'Yes, you have the receipt in your hand.'

'But it does not guarantee that it will be here when you arrive. Are you insured?

'It is something that was not, can not be insured! It is a someone not a something. My Mother's ashes.'

She just stared, a small smile beginning as she continued with the important work on the cud.

'It might have been mislaid to another flight. We will look. Please fill this in.'

Sam was handed a long form in Hebrew, Arabic and English, in which to enter all the details of the missing luggage. Just how would he describe his mother in words? He eventually handed over the completed form after thirty minutes of reading and writing., eventually passing it over, which the uniformed assistant, languidly slid towards her without reading.

'How long will it take to find it?' The assistant just shrugged and carried on chewing. 'But that box is only reason I came here.'

The assistant looked askance and stopped her gum. 'There is much to see for the tourist here. You should take in the sights.'

'I've taken them in. I just want to get my casket and do what I came here to do and leave.' As Sam said this, an armed slovenly soldier appeared at his shoulder, smiling at the assistant who smiled back at him. This was a private moment and Sam quietly removed himself from the scene.

And that was that. Sam checked in to his hotel for two days and hung around the airport, asking questions, that in answer went continually re-shrugged. Sam returned to London and Siobhan, who had already filled the space above the fire with flowers and a small ornament from the Emerald Isle.

Sam told his wife the story.

'Well, she got there. Might not be where you or your dad wanted exactly, but she is home.'

'Just one more thing I couldn't do right. She would have loved that,' remarked Sam sadly, as Siobhan hugged him, eying the 'purloined' space with satisfaction.

Croydon Beach

But just as his mother was enjoying her own self-righteous glee in ruining Sam's plans for her long awaited deliverance, Sam's dead father, Jack, supervened.

A few days later, on the Ben-Gurion airport apron, the rediscovered casket happened to fall from a transfer baggage train, in swerving to avoid a stray animal, and whilst moving other retrieved cases to the lost luggage area. After falling from the train, unseen, it had been crushed under the wheels of a jet tractor. Sam's mother spilled onto the tarmac and began to blow about in the jet wash of the El Al 747 flight bound for London. It blew and blew, swirling up into the warm night air, carrying across the airport and out towards the sea. A few miles outside the seaside town of Ashdod much of his mother's ashes met a light onshore breeze, and began to fall to earth near a tidy beach house, a substantial amount of the remainder settling unnoticed in the little garden.

Back in England that same night, staring at the vacant place his mother had left, Sam felt a strange sense of closure and completion, despite the lost urn. He happily thought of his father and his mother together in their house once more.

Croydon Beach*

These days Jack often dreamed – dreamed vividly. Dreams dismembered, remembered, re-shaped and changed each and every time: the fabric of each recollection unpicked and re-patterned in his mind. Enthusiastically he would trace the threads of un-purposed thought which wove their eager way through his mind, anxious to revisit them over and over; reworking ragged scraps into another reality – an imagined necropolis where he would roam freely and happily with old friends and comrades.

These days no one came to see Jack. Nobody telephoned or wrote to him. Important to no one, Jack was a forgotten man, forgotten by all apart from his long dead friends. These days alone in his flat he would close his eyes and let himself just drift away and into a wakeful slumber in which people from his past came to him, and increasingly he didn't have to be asleep to find himself in company. His confined solitude had become busy streets that bustled and hurried with life and where he never wanted for companions, who never grew old or agued. Even on the rare occasions when he ventured out, his phantoms would tag along chatting as they went. As long as Jack was alive, they would live – these other lives – full of undiminished youth and vigour.

'They've all gone on, Mary,' he would tell his wife yet again and she would listen quietly and patiently, smiling fondly across at her husband. In their long marriage nothing had managed to come between them, not even the death of their young son, Bobby. Jack could not even remember a time when they had once argued.

Croydon Beach

Through the years each had become the other's part – grown inseparable, holly and ivy, twined about each other – complete. Jack returned a soft smile to his wife,

'We've never let anything part us, have we dear? Remember when I said that we were so close, you couldn't get a cigarette paper between the pair of us? Remember?'

'It wasn't you who said it Jack, it was Rip at our wedding,' she gently corrected him. 'He said it in his best man's speech.'

Jack pondered, 'That's right. It was. What was it he said? Yes. Said that he could only hope that one day he would find a girl like you.' He saw her blush.

'If you are going to remember, remember it properly dear,' she chided her husband.

'Well bless my soul. Rip. Remember Rip?' Jack looked over to the window and into the leaden clouds above Croydon, which claimed to be the Manhattan of South London; smoke, that seemed to churn, impatient to enter and steal him away. He eased himself slowly from the armchair and went into the steamy kitchen to silence the call of the kettle.

'Jack, I am worried; all this not good for you,' Mary called to Jack.

'Just a minute, dear let me make the tea...?' Jack replied, as he crashed the cups and saucers. With cautious fingers, he eventually managed to remove the wrapping from the packet of shortbread biscuits and place two into each of the saucers. He filled both cups then dropped several sugar cubes into each milky tea and stirred noisily. He put the cosy on the pot and shuffled back into the sitting room and set a cup down in front of his wife. This was their little morning ritual. 'There you are my love, nice hot cup of Rosie Lee. Nice and sweet, just like you.' Jack settled back into the armchair and raised the cup to his lips gingerly sipping at the hot brew. 'Now, what isn't good for me?'

'All this thinking back about your friends and the war and such, it's not good for you.' As ever, she was looking after him. 'It's not healthy, dear.'

'Don't worry, Mary. It's only our old friends and old times. They can't hurt me. They are only memories. What else should I do?'

'Have you been to the doctor yet?' She was always more concerned about her husband's health than he was.

'There you go again, worrying. I'll get along there in good time. You just look after yourself.' He smiled and took more hesitating sips from the cup, then stopped and looked at his wife again. 'Mary, do you remember our song? How we used to sing it all the time together? First record I ever bought you. Let's see, how did it go now?' And his voice stammered along to the well-remembered words. '*No other love have I, only my love for you…only the dream we knew …no other…*' He got no further. His voice cracked and trembled and then slowly faded, something was stuck in his throat and it wasn't the biscuits.

'Oh, Jack, Jack. You lovely man,' she told him from the silver frame. 'I miss you so much.'

And he stopped singing and sat forward in his armchair wrapping his hands around the cup and stared at the picture on the sideboard; at Mary's dark grey eyes pulling him in toward her just as they had the first time they had met. He remembered taking that picture, trapping her light in that instant in which she had never grown old and was forever young. Here she was, her white floral dress yellowing from the sun, drawn into her slim waiste, its flare just drifting in the light breeze of that summer's day in Hyde Park: a hand to her hair, and her head to one side serving to emphasise the

Croydon Beach

symmetry of her shy smile. There, by the Serpentine boating lake on that first Sunday in September 1939, he could still hear her gently scolding him from the distance of all those years. 'Don't Jack, my hair's all over!' but she had smiled all the same and let him take it.

'Look at you, how beautiful you are.' He bit away a tear and looked at the ceiling. 'I still don't know what to do without you, Mary.' Jack looked again at Mary's picture, lost in her eyes once more.

'You know what to do, Jack. Course you do.'

'Rip? That you?' Jack looked around and found no one. 'You there, Rip?' Richard Ian Pullen, Rip, his oldest friend.

'You know what to do Jack,' encouraged his old friend, 'Just let go boy, it's easy. You're fourteen floors up… I was only three.'

'That's right you were.' Jack looked again at the clouds that pressed and swirled, seeing again the drifts of clearing dust and smoke from the explosion that had nearly taken his friend away that day in the barn. 'Maybe you're right.' Rip's voice was like an Angel calling him on.

'Come on, Jack boy? D'you think I'd steer you wrong?'

'Maybe I should go with you…maybe I will. I'm seeing the doctor Sheikh tomorrow, Mary said I should… The old waterworks y'know, rusting up a bit…'

'Remember, what we used to say, boy? We were just warriors for the working day… and we were in the trim.' It was the only Shakespeare Rip knew and he had made it their watchword during the war. 'Our day is done Jack, war is over, you don't have to fight any more.'

Jack got up and went over to his wife's photograph then looked across at the one next to it, like the other with its old crimped edges like lace doilies. There they were, jellied in time, beaming self-

Croydon Beach

conscious smiles out at him; Mary, Rip and Jack. He shakily picked it up and stared longingly into it, at the three of them in uniform just after the wedding, Mary's arms about the both of them, each happy for the other.

Jack was alone.

He had decided on stopping at the Welsh Harp for a Guinness. Doctor Sheikh had told him that he had been right in going to see him about his waterworks. He was going to have to have tests. 'He told me it was something to do with my postrate. Whatever that is,' he had reported to his anxious wife.

Jack settled himself into his favourite chair next to the bar and looked up at the clock for the time. The old Smiths mahogany wall clock had been replaced six years before with a large mirror advertising Jack Daniels Bourbon Old Number 7 Brand – Jack had no idea what Bourbon was or what it tasted like, he had heard of it but for him it had always been Guinness: it was, after all, good for you. But today was special for Jack; today was the 51st anniversary of Wormhoudt and the abattoir in which so many had been murdered: as he had promised himself, it was something that Jack always observed every year in memory of them.

They had been crammed into a barn after being captured from defensive positions outside of Dunkirk in May 1940, as the whole of the British and many French detachments were being evacuated by sea. They were being guarded by the 1st SS Panzer Division Leibstandarte SS Adolf Hitler division, and the SS had had a tough time of it as they were not expecting such a fierce resistance from the stout allied perimeter. They were in no mood to take prisoners after

Croydon Beach

losing many of their own comrades. There were over a hundred of them in the barn, mostly from the Royal Warwicks with some Middlesexes looking forward to POW status for the rest of the hostilities. In the afternoon the SS started tossing in stick grenades killing and wounding many. They shot several more, but a few including Jack and Rip managed to escape with superficial wounds. It was from then on that Jack and Rip became life long friends. Over eighty never made it out of the barn alive.

At the bar, he looked past the instruction to drink Jack Daniel's etched into the mirror and at himself, seeing there another face: the face of a younger man, smooth and shining, the skin burnished brightly by a different English sun. He was in uniform, his forage cap set back on his head and at an angle, a roll-up cigarette stuck behind his ear some distance below the army issue short back and sides haircut. He smiled widely and generously as, propped at the jostling four-ale bar awash with spilled beer and overflowing ashtrays, elbows and reaching arms everywhere, he waited to get served. Behind him were others in an array of uniforms from all the services; from regiments; squadrons and ships, pushing, shouting and shoving, urgent for drink. The air was a thick soup of smoke, voices and as always the piano calling on everyone to Roll out that Barrel. He held up a ten-shilling note – all he had left apart from the coins weighing down his deep trouser pocket – awaiting the return of the harassed barman behind the jump. He eventually arrived with the bottled beer and a glass.

'Sorry, Colin,' shouted Jack above the din, 'The only thing I've got that's smaller I keep for the wife.'

'It's OK Jack you don't have to yell, I've got change. And its Karl, remember, Jack?' Karl looked at Jack with concern and smiled.

Croydon Beach

'Are you OK?' he asked softly, taking the five-pound note from Jack's hand. 'Haven't seen you in here much these days.'

'No not these days, can't get away like I used to, Colin. Anyway, we're off tomorrow.' Jack tilted the bottle toward the glass and started to pour slowly and respectfully.

Karl stopped. 'Where are you off to then?'

'Where else? France of course. Just thought I'd just have a last few sherbets in Blighty before.'

'France, that's nice. Going on a day trip are ya?'

'Day trip! I should cocoa. Bit longer than that I shouldn't wonder. The balloon's gone up and we're wanted – time for my mob to be doin' our bit. And this bottle of stout is under starters orders before the off.'

'This is a bit early for you isn't it Jack? It's only 11.30.'

'Early, am I?' He looks at the mirror and finds the clock. The noise swells again drowning out the jukebox. The piano chimed and voices swelled with an open invitation to "Come and Make eyes at them down at the Old Bull and Bush". 'I've still got a few hours. Doesn't matter much …France tomorrow. Tonight'll be the last night in ol' London Town for bit. Well here's to the wife's best friend, cheers, Colin!' And Jack started to swallow the cold black liquid.

Karl shook his head. He'd keep his eye on Jack, the poor old sod. It was as if he was looking at Jack for the first time, searching the old man and trying to see just the man. He seemed different, he'd never heard him talk much, heard him mumbling to himself but not like that. Definitely going senile. As he watched the old man, mumbling and smiling over his beer, it occurred to him that if you were asked to describe an old person what could you say. The young were easy, but old people were defined by solely their age and therefore were all alike; their lives were over, they weren't interested

75

in the future only their past. Age made them invisible, their identity lost by time; known only by what they were, rather than what they are or might become. What else, thought Karl, is there to say about old people? He made himself a promise that he wouldn't end up like Jack and returned to the old fella, sliding across his change.

'Are you sure you're OK Jack?' But Jack's eyes just shone, fixed on the mirror.

'Oi, gaffer!' called an impatient voice through the other bar. 'How about it sometime today then?'

'Gotta go Jack, duty calls,' Karl told Jack, as he moved to the other bar.

'Duty calls,' whispered Jack, as he looked at his young comrades surrounding him in the mirror in their Khaki battle dresses, clamouring for as much beer as they could pack away, before shipping off to yet another war; many of them ending their short measure of days in that filthy barn, strewn and mingled with each other like so much tossed straw.

'Stella.' Jackie Burfoot pushed the money across the bar at Karl. He had just enough for one more after this. It was 11.30 and Jackie Burfoot was in trouble and he knew it. He needed money – he always needed money. Jackie needed money everyday and lots of it. His habit insisted upon it, his body demanded it. He needed some H to mellow his day, without it it was a hell of normality which was strictly for the undead, as he called them. He propped himself in the virtually empty bar of the Welsh Harp, nursing the fresh pint of lager and set himself the task of finding the source of his next score. His left heel syncopated against the barstool as he fiddled with the cigarette, trembling it in his fingers and tapping it against the edge of the ashtray. He blew the tip and it glowed then died, dead ash gathering around the point. He sneered at it then took a deep drag.

Jackie was alone.

Instead of working, Jackie had selected from the vast array of possibilities and life choices a career of indolence and thievery. Jackie didn't burgle, that required too much effort; too much work in casing places; crawling through windows; going tooled. As his particular illegitimate oeuvre, Jackie had selected street robbery, offering two options; his victims could choose a mugging with or without violence; it was entirely up to his clients. If they resisted – well it was their fault when they inevitably got hurt. He didn't want to hurt them; Jackie preferred non-violence, not out of humanitarian compassion or frail sentiment for the feelings of others, he preferred it for the same reason he didn't burgle, it was too much effort to hurt people in order to get what he wanted, but if he had to – then hey, it was all about choice wasn't it? With some self-justification, Jackie remembered Dirty Harry Callaghan's only lesson on economics. Any business, he told the class, is all about consumer choice. In Jackie's business, choice was at the centre of his offer.

    He crushed out the stub end of his cigarette and with gated fingers cupped his slowly warming lager. Then his fingers automatically moved to his mouth and he started to gnaw nervously at already chewed and raw finger nails. He knew it wouldn't be too long his before the little jags of desire would start to prick at the edges of his body. He would soon be restless, itching, then aching for the soothing balm of a fix. When it came to sourcing his habit, he had to admit to being an opportunist, never passing up the chance of gainful possibilities. Once he had been famous, albeit anonymously,

Croydon Beach

appearing as just a grainy CCTV image but seen by the whole world. It was that time the old coffin-dodger was having a seizure in the high street. He had rushed to help her as she shook violently on the pavement, shouting for someone to call 999, such was his apparent concern for the woman, he had cradled her head on his knees, covered her with his jacket whispering reassuring words into her ear: 'I'm gonna steal your fucking purse, you headcase, you old fucking nutter,' he said to her as bystanders called for help – it was so sweet. Although the eight pounds twenty-three pence didn't seem much reward for such wicked street theatre. The story had made the national news, the TV film played over and over like a repeating nightmare. The country was briefly disgusted by it, questions were asked about it, the nation searched its soul and shook its collective head over it; a nation's shame spread across the world as a symbol of Britain in moral decline. Jackie watched the coverage and read the news in open-mouthed and bemused disbelief: all that fuss over some old dying crumbly – what was the country coming to?

His eyes moved around the drab over-furnished bar, checking for possible victims – the frailer the better, less resistance equalled less effort. If it was a jungle out there, then he was the sloth: and today would be a good day for predation, for today was Thursday and Thursday was pension day.

At the age of twenty-five Jackie had long ago given up on his friends to supply him with money and his friends had long ago given up on him. His mother and father had not long since died leaving him everything they had; in return he had mercilessly divested himself of their legacy with as much thought as he had given them in their last years. They were too old to see him mature into what he had

Croydon Beach

become. A late child, long wished for and finally given them, Jackie had become what he had promised to be; a solitary; self-obsessed, needing no one and wanted by no one. As he lifted the glass to his mouth to swallow the last of the warm lager, his eyes fixed on the old'n through the other bar and instantly began to relax, it looked as if he was sorted for the day.

'Feeding time,' mumbled Jackie Burfoot, as he stared at Jack Wright's wallet, his papery fingers sorting through the meagre sum to pay for his beer.

'Oi Gaffer,' he called through to Karl, 'How about it sometime today then?'

Jack had settled to his bottle of Guinness and glanced through to the other bar catching the look of a young man who stared back. He looked a lonely, sad figure all on his own. Jack wondered how it was that you could have all that life ahead of you and not be happy at the prospect. The youngster now returned Jack's interest and grinned back as if in recognition, then slowly raised his fresh glass of lager to him. 'Why is it,' he mused, 'that youngsters today got such a bad reputation; they are no different than we were after all?' Jack smiled weakly back at the young man and tried to take a swallow of his very cold refreshed beer; it was too cold, making what remained of his teeth ache. The young lad through the bar reminded Jack of someone. Who was it? That tired young face looked so familiar. Again he started to daydream of his old comrades. He left his Guinness to get warm, too late he'd forgotten to remind Karl how he liked beer from the warm shelf, and made his way to the gents. It was strange how his memories came easily and his water painfully. He would stand and look down at the tiny pool at the bottom of the bowl that mirrored back at his shrunken cock reluctant to give up its piss. But memories were something else. They flowed and flowed in an uncontrolled incontinence of the mind. All he had to do was wait and they just swirled around him. He closed his eyes and thought of that young man in the other bar. Who did he remind him of?

'That man there! Come to attention when I speak to you, you slovenly excuse for a bombardier you!'

'Fuck off! Why? They're shooting at us for Chrissake,' reasoned the young bombardier from the relative safety of the sand.

'I'll have you on a fizzer if you don't, that's why. Now come to attention!' screamed the RSM, who had obviously seen too much, too much for any man. But Jack and Rip, unable to rise because of their wounds, watched from the shallow trench as the soldier tiredly dragged himself to a semblance of parade-ground drill. Yes, the young bombardier, that hot day in the dunes outside Dunkirk, killed right there, above them; then lying alongside them, the wounded, now dead RSM, with all his out of place swank, one on top of the other. Then Jack realised, the boy, in standing when he did, the Messerschmitt strafing run would have almost certainly hit all three of them where they had lain in the sand. The boy had saved his and Rip's lives.

'One second, youthful, alive and full of chat and cockney cheek, the next... Just like that.' They had watched that young life drain from his face and into the sand. 'What was his name? Robbie? Johnny? No. That was it, that was his name, Ronnie! How could he ever forget that boy?'

Even the most forgiving christian would find it hard to find anything redeemable in Jackie. He gave nothing and took all he could; stealing was in his nature, born to it. If there had been a star sign for thieves, he would have tried to steal it. But whatever star sign he had been born under, it had to be said he was a miracle, brought into the world much loved and longed for; what shaped Jackie was his personal journey. And as soon as he could he had started his parents on their road to dashed hope and ironic disappointment. His aged parents had idolised him, and he brutalised them for it. They built a shrine of their lives to him and he tore it down and trampled their hearts into its rubble. They lavished attention, gifts and love on him, and he took them and wanted more – always wanted more, he could never have enough. It was so easy; he just kept taking whatever he wanted.

Jackie watched, waiting for the old man to finish his drink. Still talking to himself, Jack had made up his mind to go. With trembling fingers, he slowly buttoned his coat and eased himself from the seat. He looked for Colin to say cheerio, but he wasn't to be seen, and turned to make his way out. This would be easy, thought Jackie, he stood, swallowed the remnant of his lager and stabbed out his cigarette.

The old man managed to wrestle open the heavy door and step into the street making straight for the road. Jackie left by the other door and strode over to old man waiting at the kerb.

'Hello, granddad,' said Jackie, looking at the old man and lightly taking his arm, 'Want an 'and?' Jackie's hand moved down the old geezer's back in readiness for the right moment, just push him to the ground, what harm could it do?

'That's good of you,' said Jack, 'Can't see too well these days, the sand, y'know. It's lovely to see you again,'.

Croydon Beach

'Yeah? The sand, right...? He waited and thought: One little shove, down 'e goes wallop! grab the wallet, shout for help, then away. There ought to be a law it was so easy. 'Gotta wait for the right moment Granddad, you'll be alright.'

'Jerry will be back round again soon,' warned Jack.

'Wassat, Gramps?' The old bastard had lost it. 'Who's Jerry?'

Jack smiled up at the edgy young man. 'I didn't think I would, see you again, y'know? I'm coming to attention with you Ronnie.' The old man looked up at Jackie and continued to tearfully smile at him. 'I'm coming with you, Ronnie.' Jack managed a memory of an army attention; thumbs down the line where the creases in his trousers should have been; feet at forty-five degrees.

'Who the fuck's Ronnie, now?' demanded Jackie of the old man, a mocking grin on his face.

Jack moved ahead of Jackie shaking off the young man's hand. The sand was wet and he had trouble lifting his feet. Jack started moving toward the open sea, as the Messerschmitt 109 wheeled around to begin another strafing run along the crowded shore and men ran for their lives.

'Oi, 'ang on! Where are you going? Wait, what cha doing!' shouted Jackie, as Jack went to step in front of the taxi that was barrelling down the road towards them at some speed, firing its twenty millimetre machine gun cannon as it came; Jackie reached to stop the old man, in doing so tripped and tumbled into its path as Jack fell to the pavement. The taxi ploughed into Jackie, then rumbled over his bullet riddled body like he was so much garbage.

Jack stared across the sand from where he had fallen, over at the boy whose life blood was quickly draining from his young face. Then he noticed that on his dying lips, a gentle smile began to emerge and his eyes softened as the light in them slowly dimmed.

Croydon Beach

'Thanks, Ronnie,' was all that Jack was heard to say still looking at the boy, as others lifted him to his feet and led him away up the beach to safety. 'No other love.'

Croydon Beach

Light Blue Paper and Retire

In Memorandum of Martin Slipper, Head
of Administration and Support services,
Handley, Page and Handley
1974 – 1998

From Martin Slipper
Subject: New Year 1996

May I first take this opportunity to wish all of you the very best wishes for 1996. I feel sure that the new year will bring us favourable winds and new horizons to sail toward.

This being a brand new year, I have decided, in consultation with the general office staff, that henceforth all communication between myself and all other staff shall be recorded. To this purpose, as of the 15th inst, all such communication shall be written in the form of pastelised memoranda. The new colour coding will be posted on the inter-office communications board by end of business this week.

I will of course maintain our bi-weekly meetings for which, as now, agendas will be issued for your perusal in the preceding week. (Please let me have addenda at least 24 hours before). Meetings which fall at the beginning of an accounting month will of course have the agendas dispersed one week in advance as is current practice, without addenda.

I feel sure that the new system is one of which you will approve, and in line with the forthcoming changes to Handley, Page and Handley these communiqués will be kept to the absolute minimum. In fact very much so.

To Jenny:
Subject: Memos

Jenny, can you make sure that these memos are scrupulously distributed only to those who require them. To facilitate this I have decided upon the following colour coding:

    Turquoise: Me
    Azure: All administration managers
    Pink: You
    Amber: All general Staff
    Nectarine: All other staff

Please file according to colour code and date i.e. alpha numeric. Cb 11NC would be My memo of the first of January, NC for non-confidential and so on.

Also ensure that the turquoise paper is NOT used for any other purpose than <u>my</u> memoranda.

Croydon Beach

To: Section heads
Subject: Open Door Policy

Please note the new colour coded memos. I have placed an initial order of 10 Reams of each colour with Jenny and these should be with us by week's end.

This system is crucial to the need for improved inter-staff communication through our division and indeed, if I might conjecture, the whole company.

And do please remember, all, my door is always open.

To: Bob.
Subject: Personal

Bob this is just to wish you all the best on your Masters in Business Administration and Computing final exams next week.

I know how hard you have been working and that we have all enjoyed the suggestions that you have been coming up with as a result of your studies. Some of them have been extremely amusing I must say. Those Americans and their ideas!

To: All Staff
Subject: Report Back from Neepham's

This is just to confirm that the negotiations of last year regarding the possible takeover by Neepham's is still on the cards, but very much on the back burner, and on simmer.

Neepham's management has given assurances that there will be no redundancies should the merger occur and that things will remain much as they are. Very much so.

At our meeting it was nice to see Mr. Handley in the driving seat once again after so many years in semi-retirement. Mr. Handley gave his personal guarantee that, as he put it, so long as he had breath in his body, Handley Page and Handley Associates would remain an independent company. I'm sure we can all echo that. We are very much alive and very much kicking.

To: All Staff
Subject: Mr Handley – addendum to Report back from Neepham's of yesterday

I feel sure that you like me were shocked and saddened to hear of the sudden and severe emphysema attack which took Mr. Handley from us yesterday.

The family wish no flowers, but should you so wish to pay your respects you should make a contribution to his favourite charity; The Guild for the Re-establishment of Double British Summer Time.

Croydon Beach

To: Secretarial Staff
Subject: Biscuits, tea making and other beverages

I must point out to all secretarial staff that following an unfortunate and potentially embarrassing incident regarding a visitor to this administrative floor, the provision of biscuits with tea or coffee will now be as follows:

Visitors and relations of general staff: Typhoo tea, instant coffee.
Visitors to managers: Choice of selected teas, herbal infusions and percolated coffee.
Guests of directors: as above but with a selection of biscuits, excluding Chocolate Hobnobs

These general rules must henceforth be applied with rigour, budgets as you are well aware, continue to be squeezed.

To: Secretarial Staff
Subject: Biscuits update

Please amend previous memo, Tea making and other beverages, to read: INCLUDING Chocolate Hobnobs.

To: Bob Smithers
Subject: Personal/Confidential

Let me start by congratulating you on your Masters Degree in Business Administration and Computing. I understand that you came second in the whole year, well done indeed.

Croydon Beach

I have seen the MD about your offer to take on more managerial policy responsibilities and I presented your ideas for reorganising the departments.

As I told you Bob, I am completely neutral on the subject and I neither endorsed nor rejected your, what are in my view, radical suggestions, in particular your idea regarding, as you put it, the urgent need for digitising the administration function. I simply put your ideas forward in the form of an overview.

As you are aware, times being what they are, budgets are tight. We agreed that now would not be the time to consider changes. We did however agree to look at it again in perhaps a year or so.

Your suggestions for rationalising work-flow procedures (? explanation required, Bob), I did not present to the MD as the moment did not appear expeditious. Although I did report your tenacious inventiveness in coming up with new ideas.

Keep that thinking cap firmly on and remember Bob, my door is always open. In fact VMS!

To: Deidre Shaw
Subject: My At-home

Thank you for RSVPing the invitation to the at home event with my wife and member of invited staff, which you rightly say is a welcome morale booster at this time of change and

Croydon Beach

uncertainty.

I am sorry to find that you cannot come because of your country dancing quarter finals. However, and this is difficult for me to say, but you were not actually invited and I believe you to be the victim of an office hoax. The invitation was unfortunately a forgery. You really should have been aware of this as I certainly would not have been so informal as to address you as Dear Dreary Bore.

I hope this clears it up. And good luck with those reels!

To: Bob
Subject: Re: your Memo of the 28th February
I am sorry I was unable to see you yesterday – paper work, you know how it is.

I must say I am most surprised by the vehement reaction shown by your disappointment. Contrary to your observations, I insist that I do have your interests at heart as I do all my staff. To accuse me of neglect in representing your interests fully is shameful.

If you wish to see the MD in person you may of course, that is your prerogative, but as you know he has been very busy with the Neepham's takeover. It would also demonstrate a lack of loyalty to me, a facet of your character which I did touch on with the MD.

If you wish to discuss this matter with me further, remember

Croydon Beach

my door is always open. VMS.

To: All
Subject: Holiday Entitlements

Following a meeting with the representatives of Neepham's and your Union, you may well be aware that all holiday is henceforth subject to negotiations with personnel and no longer with myself. Any queries regarding holiday arrangements should be addressed to that department.

Furthermore, ALL matters regarding salaries, time off and all related matters should also be directed to the same department.

But do please remember in these difficult and changing times under new management I am as always available to my staff and my door is always open.

To: Bill Toomey, Head of Estate Maintenance
Subject: Security

Bill, this is the third memo I have sent you regarding my door.

It is imperative that my door is able to be shut at all times and locked for obvious security reasons.

I know it's been difficult since Andy was let go, but as you and Ryan should know, we here at general admin have not been spared from the recent spate of down-sizing. In fact very much so. So come on, Bill!

To: All
Subject: Carol's departure

Well congratulations to Carol on her minor windfall on the National Lottery – well done indeed to her!

I can acknowledge on your behalf her emphatic symbolic gesture to me personally in my office following confirmation of her win. I think I know where we all stand now, well at least, I certainly do. Anyway best wishes, Carol. We shall miss her.

To: All
Subject: Envelopes

The spate of recent staff departures have led to the necessity of collection envelopes. Considering the merry whirl of changes taking place and the numbers involved I think it would be a nice touch if these could be colour coded.

Suggestions please.

And remember, out there maybe there's an envelope with your name on it!

To: Mr Robert Smithers
Subject: Staff Appraisal

Croydon Beach

Dear Mr Smithers,

As part of the appraisal procedure which has now been foisted upon us by the new management. I should like you to make an appointment through Jenny in order to expedite this procedure with due despatch. I suggest sometime next week, say Tuesday or Wednesday afternoon which ever suits you.

I would appreciate more detail on exactly how and what further information will be needed when you appraise me.

By the way Bob, belated congratulations on your appointment. I am sure we shall get on famously.

To: All
Subject: Envelope colourisation

Regarding my open invitation for envelope colouration suggestions I received only two replies. Suffice it say neither came up to the mark. In fact one was impractical, the other impossible.

There was one other suggestion which I shall be implementing, my own. As from today the suggestion box has been discontinued and removed.

Croydon Beach

To: The MD – Strictly Confidential
Subject: Workload

Dear Mr. Kane, as with the previous MD of Handley, Page and Handley with whom I had a very close informal working relationship I hope that this relationship would very much continue.

Would you favour me with a meeting to discuss my workload? You may not already be aware that my wife has not been very well recently, and these increasingly late nights and weekend meetings are becoming somewhat injurious to home life.

Perhaps we could discuss this after our next heads of section meeting.

I look forward to your reply.

To: Bill Toomey, Maintenance Staff
Subject: Toilets

Bill, I know that it's been difficult since Ryan was asked to move his career agenda to his next item and you now find yourself alone in maintenance. I'm sure he will find a job soon. I thought his dismissal a little unfair, after all magazines like that are bought by many people these days. Or so I understand.

But could you please get the gents urinals to flush properly? I personally have been drenched in, shall we say, the upper trouser area and it was most embarrassing. Whilst on the subject of toilets – Graffiti. Could you pay particular attention to references to you know what.

To: Bill Toomey, Maintenance Staff
Subject: Toilets.

I was sorry to hear about your impending dismissal. I did all that I could to arrest that decision. But as you know the management are shedding all manual direct labour and were really looking for an excuse to save redundancy payments. Unfortunately you did rather play into their hands when you were discovered spraying Graffiti in the gents.

To: The MD Confidential
Subject: Workload, your confidential memo.

Thank you for your, or rather Mr Smithers' reply to my memo regarding workload.

Can you confirm that in all matters Bob is now my conduit to you?

To: Bob
Subject: Memo's to the MD

Bob, thanks for clarifying the lines of communication enquiry.

Croydon Beach

To: All Staff
Subject: Absences

As most of you already aware since my return from the short holiday with my wife I am reinvigorated and ready for the fray. Very much so!

Thank you for your enquiries. It is nice to see that since the organisational changes my in-tray is somewhat lighter than we otherwise might have expected, the up side being I have more time for assisting staff with any personal or professional problems that may arise.

To: Jenny
Subject: Personal and strictly confidential

Just a reminder that my address is no longer The Hissops, but care-of Mr. and Mrs. Burdet, 37b Commercial Way, Maidstone.

You know all about it, so mum's.

To: Bill Toomey
Subject: Graffiti

Can I just say welcome back, Bill. I would not have expected to see you very much back in the saddle, so to speak. What a mystery how did you do it?

I must say that your memo regarding toilets and allied matters that are no longer your concern, puzzles me. Could you let me know then exactly who is dealing with the Graffiti which has now spread to the stairwells?

To: Mr Bob Smithers
Subject: Personal

I am now dealing with that certain matter we discussed and the results will be with you shortly.

(I note your request to use your full name in all further correspondence)

To: MD
Subject: Cars and the like.

I know my communications to you should go through Mr Robert S, but can I say that my company car is essential for me to carry out my functions here. And at this time would actually be personally inconvenient for me to be without a car. I know Robert supports me in this matter. Please see attached cost breakdown.

Are the rumours surrounding Bill Toomey's reinstatement true? I, for one, cannot believe someone like Toomey could get into secret societies like that.

Croydon Beach

To: Mr Robert Smithers
Subject: Memo to the MD

In line with your wishes the car will be in the car pool on Friday. I feel sure that your decision to call in my car was the right one.

Your suggestion of a bicycle is timely as my doctor suggests more exercise. Thanks for your concern.

And congratulations on the new house. I agree, three bathrooms are essential.

(Also, thank you for clarifying your preference in my not using the diminutive of your forename in all further correspondence including use of title.)

To: Bill Toomey
Subject: Graffiti

Robert has asked me to look into the increase in disgusting graffiti appearing again in the toilets, on the stairs and in the lifts. They are of a rather personal nature implicating Robert himself. Although Robert does not use any of these amenities, having his own on the top floor, he does occasionally use the lifts and stairs.

I realise that you are very busy but could you see what can be done?

Croydon Beach

To: Smithers
Subject: Malicious Rumour – <u>confidential</u>

Rumours. Look, I know what's going on. These utterly unfounded rumours about me and another member of staff are totally false and in fact could not be further from the truth.

It's you isn't it? You have never liked me have you? Fair enough so you got the job you wanted. People like you are the coming thing is that right? Professional management with your MBAs and your personal marketing skills. Well you can have the lot. You have assisted in wrecking my marriage and stolen my self-esteem, and everything I have ever worked for.

And in case you should like to talk *de hombre a hombre* you can forget it because that would flatter one of us – it would probably flatter you, now, wouldn't it?

Let's not mince words, I now have the guts to say this. Bob, you are a heartless self serving bastard! Oh yes you are! With your neat suits and matching ties and your sincere yet determined, "I-am-in-control-of-my-destiny" look.

You stole my job. I have lost my wife. I have lost my house, even my car, yes, you even took my car. I have nothing left. Just more time to contemplate my life's vacuum. I hope there is a God, and he is an angry and vengeful God.

I am mad as hell and I am not taking anymore. Very much so.

Croydon Beach

FOR PERSONAL FILE ONLY, NOT SENT

To: Bill Toomey
Subject: Graffiti

Bill, just to let you know all the Graffiti has been removed from the stairwells and toilets as per your instructions. Sorry that I took so long, it was quite a tricky job and I kept swooning from the chemical smells in the confines of the stairwell.

To: All
Subject: Me

Since the amalgamation of the administration section into Logistics and Planning, (those Americans and their ideas!) and after all we have been through together, this would be an ideal time to wish you all the best in your new endeavours.

We are fewer than we were, but we happy few, we band of brothers and sisters, we are none the worse for all that.

Just to let you know that I shall be staying here to wind things up and then, who knows?

To: Bob
Subject: Personal

I know what you are doing, I just want you to know that. I hope you get what's coming to you. I don't care what you do

Croydon Beach

to me now, you have done your worst. I hope you are proud of yourself.

It was you who got Bill Toomey to write the Graffiti wasn't it? That's why after he was fired by the MD you got him his job back. And tried to cover it up by writing stuff about yourself.

Size isn't everything you know! Or maybe you think it is.

DO YOUR WORST, YOU HEARTLESS BASTARD!

To: all
Subject: My finale

Thank you very much for the gift. This as you already know will be my valedictory memo.

I would very much like to attend a farewell drink at The Grape and Grain but please accept my apologies I have to decline, I'm sure many of you will be pleased to hear. I know I was not popular with many of you, but I did my best for the company and, I hope, by all of you.

So thank you for the invitation, it was very kind. But tonight I shall be winging my way to a well earned pre-retirement sunshine holiday with my new partner. Yes, I am retiring, far, far too young, I know.

I can only wish you all the luck in the world. As you may well know my wife and I are now divorced and I shall be left with a

Croydon Beach

small early taken adequate pension and as I shall only be responsible to myself and my partner, I shall enjoy life in the round and forget the detail.

To All, and copied to the board of directors:
Subject: A Final Memo from Ibiza, Spain

Thanks for not deleting my email account, which allows me to send this postcard memo from the first day on our hotel's private beach.

To Bob in particular I would like to say how hard it must be to accept the heavy burdens of management especially in these rationalising times. Some of your decisions have made you very unpopular, all the more so since having risen from the ranks you made many of your colleagues, once considered friends, particularly embittered.

I know you have been putting in extra hours and weekends over the last year or more, and even with your move to an even larger house, these responsibilities can put a strain on any seemingly perfect relationship; how one's personal life always suffers as I found to my own personal cost.

But Bob, every cloud... they say. When you suggested getting a bicycle to replace the car, who could have foreseen the consequences? Well perhaps you should have seen this one. With all your forward planning and insights, isn't that one of modern management's functions after all?

Croydon Beach

"Get a bike," they say "and improve your sex life." So I did, I got a bike. I got fitter, got out of Maidstone and got around to your lovely house and got to meet your charming wife. I have found a new vigour in life and I am going to share it.

Just to let everyone know, that I called on your wife, Bob and she showed me round your new home. I swore her to secrecy about my calling, and calling, you could actually say, became a regular occurrence over the next weeks and months. Over the long weekends, when you were at your work, all those long hours and days, we found a mutual interest in each other. She is my silver lining, Bob.

We explored your house from every angle in every room, especially the three bathrooms. And did so regularly, together and may I say, exhaustively.

If I could offer one piece of advice, to never get bogged down in detail. I once said that you were only doing what the job dictated. But you cannot separate the man from his actions. You were not just obeying orders, you took delight in what you did.

So, let's hear it for all those unsung folks who have been unfairly treated, abused and dismissed as unworthy to fit into the scheme of things that have become what they truly are: an age of rage.

Oh, and Bob, on case you haven't had time to find it, your wife's light blue farewell memo is on the mock Victorian

Croydon Beach

mantelpiece next to the picture of yourself with your arm around the MD.

In closing, may I say, good luck to nearly all of you and can I remind staff that the drinks machine no longer accepts bronze coinage. In fact, very much not!

Martin

Croydon Beach

The Fairy Godfather
A Bull City Tale*

Between heaven and hell.
Between Jehovah and Jesus
Between Lexington and 5th
Between Life and Death
Between the bagel and the bullet
Between the bullet and the muzzle
Between muzzle and muzzle tov
Between the shot glass and the shot
Between the pistol and the Don
Between the Don and his future
   … stepped Howard.

Bismarck

Maybe it wouldn't be the last time he saw Maddy, but just then to Howard it sure did feel like it was going to be. He stared into the sun after her bus as it sped out of Bull City on a carpet of dust and heat haze. Howard was on the top of his roof watching until the Greyhound to Bismarck reached the town limits. He watched it pass the abandoned remains of Pete and Nadine Kolinski's place, then, near its rusting and barely turning wind pump, it slowed, gunned its engine once and without stopping turned left onto Interstate 94 and accelerated into the gathering distance. His wife was finally on her

Croydon Beach

way. She would be at Bismarck airport in two hours. After a half-hour wait and if it all went to schedule, she'd be on the North Western flight to New York and one hour later on the KLM redeye to London Gatwick. Maddy would be back in England around sunrise local time – it was that quick.

He had wanted to drive her to Bismarck but she had insisted on the bus, saying that she might as well get used to doing things for herself again - '*At least for a while, Howard*'. On his journey home from the bus station, Howard had given this some further thought and wondered again at what she had meant about getting along without him: doubts about her promise of return started to bob to the surface of his thoughts like dynamited fish. After their goodbyes he had kicked the complaining Toyota flatbed the mile and half back to their two story Colonial style house in quick time. He dived out of the truck and leaving the engine running, made the ladder two rungs at a time just managing to climb onto the flat roof and get that last sight of the Greyhound. She had been the only one to get on the bus and no one got off. People rarely got off the bus at Bull City, unless it was for a comfort break or to grab a coke to slake a dusty thirst on their way somewhere. Sometimes they got off by mistake – it was an error Maddy was finally rectifying.

Bull City was defined by its crossroads – the town's history had been determined by the relationship between two prairie highways which briefly encountered each other and very quickly went their separate ways. Anyone looking hard enough could find Bull City on a Rand McNally road map looking like a small dirty X; an illiterate's signature scratched on the featureless land by weary cattle drovers and hopeful pioneers. It marked the spot which once, for a while and long ago, beckoned with the promise and dreams of a better life. Beyond it lay the Dakota Badlands and Bull City was where wagon

Croydon Beach

trains stopped to draw breath before plunging further and deeper west. Cattlemen driving their huge steer herds toward the cities in the East, crossed trails with settlers straining westward in their oxen yoked Schooners. Nothing much ever stuck in Bull City, it was a place built for passing through.

Following the Greyhound's progress, Howard captured the shrinking silver bus between his thumb and forefinger and squinted at it, slowly closing the gap between them as it shrunk. When they touched he lowered his hand and then his head. The late morning heat of the roof was suddenly oppressive, bearing down on him as if it had a weight more substantial than just air. It pressed out the feeling that he had said goodbye to more than his wife. Something else had gone with her, something to do with childhood, the merest memory trace of some precious loss, something he couldn't quite locate. From the roof he looked down at the aerial plan of their piece of earth. The yard with its untended shrubs and long weeds barely concealing the camouflaged remains of a World War Two Willis Jeep he'd bought to fool around with, its army green and white star fading in the sun. Spreading its shade over half the yard the Nuttail Oak dangled its single fruit from a piece of mildewed tow-rope; lashed to its end, the tyre-swing whispered against the tall spears of uncut rye grass as it moved in an imperceptible breeze.

He forced his fingers into his jeans back pockets and looked at the crazy patchwork of tar paper beneath his feet he had been constantly altering over the years, trying to keep the rain from getting in. He grinned to himself as he thought back to when he had first shown it to Maddy and told her that he was making a huge map of the western United States, so that it could be seen from passing aeroplanes. He explained that from high up you could make out at least eight of them with their regular state lines and just there, surrounding the furnace flue, was the shiny black outline of North Dakota. She had believed him. It was the only time she ever went up there – this was Howard's realm. Every time the roof leaked, up he would climb, up there to seal it again. Tracing the border of one of the states with the toe of a huge chain-saw boot, Howard idly pressed down a blistering edge of old tarred paper which popped up a few inches away. He stamped on the bubble and the mastic seam instantly separated exposing dark bare timber beneath.

'Ah, Gosh darn-it!' Another repair. He looked out towards distant Lake Tschida, out to where the bus had finally disappeared and thought of their short marriage. To Howard that roof was a lot like it, he was always there patching and mending, and lately it had got so that it seemed he was up there most of the time, trying to stop stuff getting in. Howard hunkered down in a corner of the hot roof and leaned his back against the parapet; he drew his knees up, rested his bare forearms on them and loosely swung his hands. He let his head fall back and looked up, Bull City had disappeared – all he saw was sky, huge and empty and frightening. He shivered. He had never felt so alone.

Patrick Dacey

Dacey's bar is a place that never answers any questions – it's a place that takes you in no matter who you are as long as you are buying. Dacey will listen and will never judge or offer advice. He will polish glasses, draw beer, register your cash – it's cash only by the way – refresh the pretzels bowl and wordlessly agree about the pitcher's arm or the batter's average, whatever. He didn't talk because he didn't have to. The only thing that came across his bar that interested him was cash money.

Croydon Beach

'Hey, you hear about that guy on the heights; went home totally soused, killed his wife after she wouldn't let him rock the Kasbah? Turns out he'd got into the wrong house and killed the wrong wife. His wife was waiting home for him ready for his Friday night special. Now ain't that a kick in the head? I tell ya, these condos all look alike and it gets so the wives all look alike too.' For Dacey tales like that would nearly always miss their mark. Dacey would merely move his match from one corner of his mouth to the other. That was about the only comment you'd get; Dacey was eloquent with matches that way.

Howard had stumbled along Lexington and had strayed into Dacey's which did a fine line in Bourbon straight up with a twist and a beer to chase it all the way to the spot – where it invariably and really did hit. After two years alone, Howard had decided not to follow his wife to London, England. His neighbour Vern had finally convinced him she was gone and wasn't about to come back to him. The postcards had dried up after six months, and he hadn't heard from her since that last one, which had read, 'Love Julie.' Was it an instruction? The picture on the card was of strange looking guys in red uniforms and black pancake hats standing outside a castle. Apparently they liked eating steaks.

In the bar, Howard had been telling Dacey about how his English wife, after leaving him then divorcing him, had hooked-up with some long cocked, short selling futures manager over in London, England. Then he'd showed Dacey his manuscript, thick with pages and thin on insight. Here was his life story, a Bull City Tale and his way back, or so he thought; the script for his dream of America that he had tried naively to hawk around the brutish publishing houses of New York his trip paid for by some of the good folk of his native Bull City. He slapped the heavy tome.

Croydon Beach

'Two years Patrick, two years and all I've got to show for all the faith my little town put in me is right here on your bar soaking up the beer spills. What do you think about that?'

Mick Dacey didn't mind being called Patrick, it was his favourite saint, the way he'd rid Ireland of all those slimy SoBs from this sad guy, kindly guy, he didn't mind at all. He just switched the match from right to left and back. Howard watched Dacey's eyes for approval, detected a small glint in the left one and took this for acknowledgement.

'Yeah, you're right! Gosh darn it! When you're right, you're right,' returned Howard, acknowledging the glint. 'Gimme a double shot, will ya now, me Bucko? Something out of my ordinary.' Howard's last George Washington note and change fell flat on the bar. Dacey scooped up the last of Howard's money and without looking, registered that there was not enough even for a single. Howard swayed away gripping the edge of the bar to keep him in the vertical. Dacey poured him a double and slid it in front of Howard. He watched as Howard started to down it like a man on the very edge of life.

The first half disappeared. 'Back to Bull City and the reception party. Lucky I still got my ticket anyways for the overnight train. Gotta get to Grand Central. Beautiful station you have there to be sure, beautiful,' explained Howard, before downing his drink to last drop and making to leave. 'Ah well, t'anks Patrick, you played the Irishman true and sure, begorah.' Dacey almost grinned at Howard's attempts at the Oirish.

Dacey, never known to speak unnecessarily with his clients, removed Howard's shot glass and wiped away its history, then removed his match. To the regulars he looked suddenly naked.

'Hey Howard, you take care, you hear me? You take care,'

Croydon Beach

called Dacey as Howard went the long route to the door. Other drinkers looked at Dacey, then at the disappearing Howard, trying to figure what was so special about the drunk that such blessings and unusual eloquence are heaped upon him. But Howard hadn't heard Dacey's, as it turned out, prescient, warning; he was through the door not registering the reaction of the other customers who had never heard Dacey speak so much or so fulsomely.

Howard stumbled from Dacey's clutching the precious manuscript to his chest and pulling at his chunky suitcase. Outside he tripped and fell straight into a well dressed man he hadn't seen. The both of them tumbled to the sidewalk just as the gun spoke and it spoke loud and fast. The nervous gunman clicked bullets around like it was incense at an orthodox wedding. People ducked and dove or stood amazed. Glass smashed; cars rammed each others as mayhem escaped. The first shot missed Isaac by inches as did the second and the third. Others came to rest in a dog; a lady's fur collar, it's fox shot for a second time; a discarded Big Kahuna Double Cheese Burger lunch box, going through the meat coming to rest amongst the fries and salad; through an open window, and through the bathroom door laying waste to a perfectly good bottle of Crystal mouthwash; through a windshield of a Ford Impala '78 and into the recently restored duck-egg blue upholstered leather seat; into a flagpole, patriotically missing its flag; and the last, finally exhausted, seriously wounded a warm salmon and cream cheese bagel just being served across the counter at the Famous Bagel and Beef Kosher Food Bar on 5th Avenue. The ones that found human flesh found only Howard's.

The assassin fled thinking his job done, having watched the Don tumble to the ground under his hail of his bullets. As he ran to his car, he saw his future; elevated in the clan; feted by his new bosses; the best tables at restaurants and girls all over him; he saw himself stretched out in the back of a shiny stretched limousine – it would be a pity that he couldn't have seen himself eventually and inevitably stretched out in the back of a shiny funeral parlour limousine.

Isaac had fallen to the ground his body covered with Howard's drunken limp mass of wounded humanity. Not feeling the bullets now residing in his drunken body all he could say was:

'Oops. Sorry buddy. Didn't see you there. You OK? Here, I...lemm...lemme help you up?' But he was in no state to even help himself, able only to roll off the Don and into the gutter. He hadn't even noticed the blood leaking from his wounds. When he did, he looked at it as the handyman in him did and said just before he lost consciousness:

'It's OK, lady, I can fix that leak for you for couple of bucks,' as his lifeblood, and remnants of the vomited liquor flowed down a nearby drain.

Issac the Don

At the age of 73 he had his family, all of whom respected Don Isaac, and none of whom were directly related. He was a small man who spoke softly because he wanted to; slowly and carefully because he could and carried a big pistol because he needed to. But the Don killed people only when he had to; he was fair that way, and to be fair, had to – a lot.

Now, as his allotted time rolled around, as it does for all, he began to take a hard honest look at his life. He wondered if the adopted Italian son of a pair of Jewish refugees could ever be allowed into a comfortable afterlife after all he had done. He had decided to

Croydon Beach

retire and to make his peace with God. At the same time, one of his family had also decided he should be retired, and for Isaac to be with his God sooner than he would wish to be.

So here he was, standing on the sidewalk of Lexington and 5th outside of Dacey's Irish Bar looking across the street at the B'nai Jeshurun of Jassey Synagogue, then over to St Anthony's Catholic church next to it, and back, undecided as to which God and heaven he should go to and ask forgiveness and redemption. As he contemplated his dilemma, the edgy assassin closed in. Maybe he could go to both, insurance for a life of murder, drug dealing and thievery; it seemed the only course that contained any certainty.

The assassin for his part in all of this, was set on his way by casual remarks between two of Isaac's lieutenants. He had overheard them telling each other that they had both had wished him well for his last birthday. The ambitious assassin had taken that to mean that they had wanted it to be his very last birthday. The Don's death would inevitably lead to his personal promotion in the ranks.

He removed the PEPTIC 4.6 from his coat pocket and slipped the safety off, pulling the barrel back, the round entering the firing chamber. A sweaty finger wrapped itself around the cold trigger. The firing pin waited, urgent to get on with its purpose. And for the hit man as well, this was his waited for moment.

Howard Awake

So there he was waking up. Waking up as only a really committed drinker knows. He was conscious but his eyes were still clamped, eyelids the only baulk against the insisting light on the other side. Everything in Howard's head was pink-red, he was in a womb and whoever it was, had a powerful searchlight playing on the belly ball

Croydon Beach

outside.

Inside he examined himself for pain – for pain there would certainly be. Where was it hiding? Oh yeah, there it was. It made his breath hitch. Somewhere behind his eyes, between his ears was the presence, digging in for the duration, like marines in a foxhole preparing for the main bombardment; a scorpion in the mind holding on waiting for a movement, any movement to detect its prey, then over would come the stinging rebuke. Howard winced, his eyes screwed tight, the cervix dilating in spasms, then contracting somer, trying to push him into the light, to force open his eyes, slap him awake once more and scream out a new life, a new day. Howard resisted.

Then he was aware of another presence. What could this unfamiliar visitor be? Howard fidgeted, then someone hit him in his ribs. But the pain did not go, whoever had hit him was now sitting on his chest, crushing out his breath. He opened his mouth to breathe and drew in what he could, but it hurt so much he screwed his eyes even tighter. Still it did not go; whoever was sitting on his chest began levering under his ribs with what he guessed must be a spoon, gouging at the meat like the centre of a juicy rib-eye steak. He was hurting and he now wanted the world to know. He pulled in as much air as the weight on his chest would allow and from deep inside the centre of his being began a crescendo scream. Low at first getting nearer and higher in its pitch, until it was near enough for his voice to give it enough air. And the howl was shot out of him and sent on its way. His eyes opened – and CRASH – in came the light and the world streamed in with it. He was reborn into a world of pain.

A hospital room; a ceiling; a window; machines and tubes and the smell of flowers and formaldehyde; light, noise and more pain – it wouldn't stop. A man leaned in, followed by a piercing light increasing the pain. He waited inside – waiting for the doctor to tell his mother: 'Congratulations, it's a fine boy. And by the looks of him a strapping lad all of 230 pounds.'

And there he would be at his mother's breast, drinking, drinking, downing that temperate liquid with its reassuring hint of Jack Daniels, until, once more, into grateful unconsciousness he would return. But no, there was that pain again, and another in his leg and yet another in his foot. His hangover was spreading to hitherto remote and exotic places. There was a drip in his arm, the gauge being turned by the black white nurse. Howard squinted up at the beaming smile.

'There he is. You're awake.' The nurse turned back from the white black doctor and smiled, 'We haven't lost you then?'

'Better up the dose, nurse. The pain should begin to ease now, Mr. Stoneman. Let us know if there's anything else you need. Anything at all. And don't worry about insurance cover, that's all been taken care of.'

But all Howard could focus on was the white coat hanging on the doctor's narrow shoulders. He looked at the buttons and thought in that practical way of his: 'Could there be anything more useless than buttons on a doctor's white coat. You never see 'em done up do ya? I mean, what's the point?'

Then Howard felt a warm stream flow through his body. He was on a boat sailing away to his own personal and distant shore. The hurt started to recede. Then he was in bed being tucked up again, a child of seven maybe eight, his mother chasing away the pain of mumps with her soothing balm until it didn't hurt anymore.

'Thanks, Mom,' he heard someone say. He couldn't believe how quickly he had grown. But it didn't matter, he was safe, warm, and people cared about him.

Croydon Beach

Howard wakes a second time.

Howard was growing up fast. The next time he awoke he was a hero.

He was being hugged, kissed and he didn't like it. There was garlic on those lips – a fragrance he was a stranger to, never having eaten anything more foreign than Kentucky fried chicken; that being its exotic and distant country cousin from Maryland. Under-lacing the garlic was a strong hint of lavender- musk – he started to feel queasy.

'Here's the boy I never had. Look at him.' His cheeks were pinched and he grimaced. 'Nothing, nothing is too good for my boy here. You hear that? Nothing. Anything he needs you give it to him. The best.' As the smells diminished a little, Howard decided to focus and was about to speak when whiskery lips met his full on and in an effort to pull away succeeded in rending one of his sutured wounds and he once more fell into a deep dreaming sleep. He hadn't even seen what his father looked like. Howard slipped back into sleep anxious to rid himself of the dream he had just had and return to his beautiful shore.

When he woke the final time. The pain was much reduced. He tried to sit up and look around. The room was huge, with a sofa, armchairs, paintings on the wall. It was light airy with a huge window. Was he in a hotel? Bestrewn around the room and covering every horizontal surface, were flowers of all kinds. On the large side table sat his manuscript. He reached for it, causing him some discomfort. There, right through the O of his first name, was a bullet hole. Apparently after forensics had done with it, it had been returned to Howard, almost certainly unread. On the rear of the manuscript was a continuation of the hole and blood stains. He stripped away his bed sheets and matched the line of the hole to where he had been hugging it when the bullet hit. The book had slowed to bullet's velocity enough to save his life but not enough to stop it entering his chest.

He found the call button and it seemed within seconds someone was in the room asking how they could help. Anything he desired, was the order of the day.

The next day, announced by a rather large man in a dark suit, Howard would soon be in the presence of a rather important personage. He at first thought it could be an early repeat visit by his surgeon. However, he did not recall the suited man in the unnecessary dark glasses and a sharp suit announcing his visit. After ten minutes with the big guy staring at Howard, the doors opened and in flounced a rather small man. He was beautifully attired, and almost immediately the room was filled with the overpowering aroma of lavender-musk once more.

'Hey,' he called, as another big guy outside the room stood watch 'There he is, my boy. He shrugged off his coat from around his shoulders, which was neatly taken by dark glasses man, carefully folding the precious thing over his arm. Isaac moved to Howard's side and sat never taking his squinty eyes from him.

'Can I help you?' asked Howard.

'Will you listen to him? Can he help me, he says,' announced the Don, looking around for an audience. 'After what you did? I'm here to help you. You schlamiel Howard, I'm here to help you. What's this?' He picked up Howard's book and looked at the bullet hole it was sporting. 'This is how you did it right. Boy, went straight though before it got to you, huh?'

Croydon Beach

'But look fella, just who are you? The police? If you are, I can tell you now, I don't know how I got here, apart from the fact I got shot outside a bar.'

'That's my boy! That's my Howard,' he looked around for his audience again. Dark glasses man was unmoved. 'Let's keep it like that, OK? We have ways of taking care of things ourselves, we don't need to get the cops involved any more than we have to, right?'

Isaac went on to explain to Howard how he was in the hospital after having three bullets removed from his body.

'So you can see what you did.'

'Really? Is that what happened? Wow.'

'Come on don't be coy. Will you listen to yourself? Don't you get it? I owe you my life, and I am seeing to it you will be handsomely rewarded. And here is the first.' From a bag he was carrying he slowly and theatrically pulled a present, with bright ribbons tied very professionally around colourful paper. Howard unwrapped it, and there was a hardback book. Howard tried to focus on the title: 'Bull City Tales: Stories from a Small American Town. By Howard Stoneman', it read. He gripped the book in both hands. Was he still dreaming? He flicked the pages.

'The publishers are telling me it's something called a proof copy and that it has been edited and awaiting your final approval before distributing internationally. I had the original put back there for you yesterday,' explained the Don.

'But how did...?'

'Ehhh... some people owe me favours, and let's say I have very persuasive ways in showing them where our mutual interests might lie. So my boy, what do you want to do with the remaining two?' Isaac waited, grinning below his perfectly symmetrical mini moustache. 'Any ideas yet?'

Croydon Beach

'Other two? Other two what? Mr er...?' Howard was still reeling from the book news, still looking at his name.

'Just call me Mr Bergstein,' replied Isaac.

'Bergstein? That name sounds Jewish, but you sound a little New York Italian.'

'It's a long family story. Families eh, what cha gonna do with them? So now, the other two. You got one for the book, and you still got another two. Any thoughts just now?' He grabbed Howard's hand and held it lightly. Howard could feel the smooth skin on his. This was a man who did not do physical labour. Howard was still looking mystified.

'OK, look, lemme explain. You took three bullets for me, right? So, for each one you get a favour returned. One for the book right there and two more to come.'

'What sort of favours?'

'Well...anything, anything that is in my powers I can do for you, that is. Look, take it easy. Relax. Have a think. I'll be back in a couple of days to see how you're doing. There's someone I need to take personal care of in the meantime,' he said looking thoughtful. 'Maybe you'll have a few ideas by then.'

'You could sort some guy out for me, over in London,' joked Howard. 'Stole my wife.' He tried to chuckle.

'Oh yeah?' The Don looked seriously interested. 'Who might that be?'

But the pain was starting to kick back in and he winced.

The Don pressed the call button and with seconds his bed was surrounded with a phalanx of attending medicos.

'I'll see you in a couple of days, OK? And make sure he gets everything he asks for.' he said patting his hand twice more, nodding knowingly to the doctors. He rose and quickly flounced out of the

Croydon Beach

room, dark glasses man wrapping his coat back around his shoulders as he left, and taking his lavender-musk with him. Everyone in the room breathed easier, except Howard.

Outside he spoke to his bodyguards telling them to start the ball rolling on the guy over in London England; Howard wanted taking out for the second of the Don's promised favours. Heavenly salvation for Isaac would have to wait a while longer until that third favour was fulfilled for his earthly saviour and good friend, Howard.

*Bull City Tales – To be published 2022

Croydon Beach

The Renaissance of Rennie Sutcliffe

Rennie Sutcliffe woke one morning feeling very odd. She had had a very late night the evening before, returning home after nine PM. and immediately retiring to her bed. As she lay awaiting sleep, she reflected on the evening out she'd had with her friends – Molly, Doreen and Amy. They'd stayed out later than usual after the weekly afternoon bingo at the church hall. Molly had won the main prize, twenty-five pounds, and had treated them all to supper at her small flat.

The four had been the best of friends for longer than any of them cared to remember, indeed, could remember. Their interests had grown together over the intervening years. But now it seemed that all their conversations consisted largely of exchanging views of their various aliments, the curse that went with the great ages they had all been blessed with.

'It's my teeth, they just cannot seem to get my top plate right. It's still loose. I complain, but what's the good?' asked Molly of her friends, that post bingo evening. Teeth were a regular topic for their deliberations.

'That Mr Mahmood,' enjoined Amy, 'not as good as Mr Jenkins.' This she said shaking her head sagely to which the others, apart from Rennie, grumbled out agreement.

'Shame he's a darkie dentist,' added Doreen, as a considered afterthought. 'I don't like those fingers around my mouth. Gives me the shivers, it does. Ooh, no!'

Croydon Beach

The rest of the early evening, consisting of tea and bought cakes, continued in this vein, all four exchanging grumblings common to the elderly.

However, complaints about how things had gone down hill since 'all the migrants' was something Rennie refused join in with. For it would have seemed to an outside listener, that somehow their deteriorating health was somehow paralleled with, and causal of, the arrival of foreign, mostly dark-skinned, medics.

Each of them talked fulsomely about their latest and continuing mysterious ailments, which the doctors could not seem to find a cause for, apart from that chestnut:

'It's your age,' the doctors would inform them, raising their voices that were edged with that special slow patronising emphasis reserved for the elderly. 'At your age, you should expect that things will go wrong a little. Yes?'

'Still, what do they know? Doctors!' And three of the four would agree and reach for another iced bun, or rich tea biscuit, softening them up in the hot tea from Molly's prewar china tea service. The service that had survived the bomb that had taken her husband and house, but spared the china, with not a chip or scratch. All the while Rennie would listen politely and occasionally putting in a word after much deliberation. She was not one to rush to judgement about anyone, happy enough to talk about health, something common to them all; something that fused their friendships.

'I suppose though, it's only to be expected,' suggested Rennie, gently. 'None of us are getting any younger are we? If only we could! That would be nice, wouldn't it?'

To this, of course, they would all readily agree. She, for her part, liked Mr Mahmood. He was a rather nice, kind man. But this she never confided to her friends. The evening was going too well to be spoiled by disagreement or controversy, something they always seemed to avoid whenever they were together.

In the yellow light from the street streaming through the thin curtains, Rennie's eyes tried to focus on the ticking clock on her side table, where resided her pills, glasses and hearing aid. She could just make out that it was around eleven o'clock and sleep still eluded her. She turned slowly in her bed and tried find a comfortable position where her chronic arthritis could be the least painful. As she lay there drifting off into sleep, her mind reimagined her youth, recalling what she told her friends earlier:

'None of us are getting any younger are we? If only we could! That would be nice, wouldn't it?' What would she give now for another time of that youth? She mused. But what had she to give?

Late next morning found Rennie at the opticians, after persuading the receptionist that she needed an emergency appointment. Following that she was advised to see her doctor as a matter of some concern.

'Good Morning Rennie, what can we do for you? How are you managing the arthritis?'

'Yes, thank you Doctor. It's that and other things I've come to see you about.' Rennie liked Doctor Chevapravatdumrong; liked her soft manner and concern. Her friends tried to avoid her. They had taken a dislike to her name which they grew tired of trying to pronounce and just called the smaller woman Dark Doctor, or just a lazy – Doctor Cheva; this despite her years of devoted service to the community, her patients and their personal welfare.

'Well, it's all a bit strange really,' replied Rennie, 'and I am very worried by it all, Doctor.'

Croydon Beach

'Oh dear. What is troubling you?' asked Doctor Chevapravatdumrong, she smiled and tried to set her patient at ease. For she in turn liked Rennie, reminding her of her own mother in Sri Lanka, whom she had not seen for many years. Her practice took up all her time, as it was short of two GPs, and exhausted though she was, she just could not find enough time to visit her family in Tangalle.

Regarding the good doctor, Rennie for her part couldn't see for the life of her why the others disliked her. They knew that Rennie always saw the good in people, always seeing the positive side of anyone; she was kind, considerate and generous in all her dealings with people; it was something that seemed for some reason, to irritate her friends. This gentle forgiving nature of Rennie endeared her to the doctor. And as she grew older and the afflictions of old age piled up, new ones nudging the older ones along to take up residence in her ageing body, the doctor would do what she could to help, ameliorate and console.

'It's about what happened yesterday. At Boots.'

'The chemists?' asked Doctor Chevapravatdumrong.

'Chemist, yes. No. At the optician. I had to get an emergency appointment. They were so kind. Always so considerate.'

'What happened at Boots then?' she leaned toward Rennie, encouraging her with a soft smile.

'Well, yesterday, I woke up after a really good night's sleep. The like of which I haven't had since, well, since I can't remember. When I woke I felt so... refreshed. It was very strange.' Rennie waited for a reaction from the doctor who just knitted her brow and continued to listen, so encouraged Rennie to go on with her tale uninterrupted.

'Anyway, normally I take my glasses from the side table and

Croydon Beach

put them on to see the time and well, I just couldn't see a thing. Everything was blurry. It was odd, I could see better without them. I was so worried I almost called you straight away, but I didn't want to worry you. Instead I called Boots and they got me in that morning after I told them what had happened. They were so kind.'

The doctor's smile widened at Rennie's generous spirit to people just doing their job. 'OK, I see. So what happened at Boots?' She loved listening to the old girl, loved to hear her amusing stories, when she was in the mood to tell, and usually she was, today wasn't one of those days.

'He tested my eyes, and told me that my cataracts no longer needed an operation. That my eyesight was twenty something?' Rennie looked mystified, her clear hazel eyes asking for assistance.

'Twenty-twenty? Really? Is that what he said?'

'That's right. He said I had perfect vision. That's why the glasses weren't working. He said I didn't need them any more.' Rennie and the doctor were both quiet, each looking at the other quizzically, wanting for answers from the other; the doctor not quite knowing what to say. Rennie continued. 'Yes. He said to give you this. I think it's the examination thing he gave me. He said I should show it to you. So here I am.'

'Doctor Chevapravatdumrong, took the paper and read it. Still speechless, after reading the optician's report, she reread Rennie's medical history as the old lady sat waiting patiently for the doctor's attention. The record there betrayed the calamity of such a long life. Eighty three and waiting for a double hip operation; crippling arthritis that was distorting the long fingers of her doubtless once delicate hands into cruel shapes of discomfort and pain. Her sight failing; deafness and heart murmurs. All of which the gods had given this kind old lady, bringing such a heavy burden crashing down upon her. And now it seemed there was emerging evidence of onset dementia. The doctor slowly shook her head at the optician's report, an oblique smile on her tired face.

'He says here that he booked you in for a hearing test after the eye exam?'

'Yes, he did.'

'And how are you doing with the medication, Rennie?' asked the doctor, slowly and deliberatively, raising her voice close to Rennie's best ear, to check what the audiologist had added to the letter.

'Oh,' she exclaimed, pulling away from the doctor.

'What's the matter?' asked the doctor, 'are you in pain?'

'No. It just that your voice is very loud. Are you shouting?'

'Yes, but I...,' began the doctor, a look of confusion returning to her face. 'I'm sorry.' The doctor sat back. 'Would you mind if I asked a colleague to come and see you.'

'I want you as my doctor.'

'No, I would like her to give me a second opinion, that is all.'

'You have me worried now.'

'There is no need, Rennie. There is nothing to worry about. In fact it seems quite the opposite.'

'My hearing is the other reason I have come to see you. Everything is so loud. The neighbours and their young children and what they got up to last night in their bedroom. I could hear it all. Kept me awake, and the television… well. Apart from that, I am sleeping so well, it's like a real tonic. What's happening to me, doctor?' A look of deep concern occupied Rennie's otherwise kindly face.

'OK. Look, let's get Doctor Mason to come in. Is that all right?'

'Yes, of course, doctor. Anything you say.'

Doctor Chevapravatdumrong left the room leaving Rennie with her thoughts. She returned shortly with Doctor Mason.

'Hello, Rennie. Is it OK if I ask you some questions alongside Doctor Chevapravatdumrong?'

'Of course it is, doctor.'

'Rennie, can I ask? Do you have any pain in your hands?'

'No, I don't, now you ask.'

Doctor Chevapravatdumrong indicated Rennie's hands to Doctor Mason which had straightened and become more flexible and dexterous.

'Tell Doctor Mason what you told me about your glasses and the optician. Go ahead, Rennie, please.'

'Well, she told me that my eyes, I mean, had cleared up. Said she had never seen anything like it.'

Mason sat back in her chair, totally perplexed after reading the report from Boots. 'Can I have look in there, Rennie? Would that be all right?'

'Of course, doctor.'

Doctor Chevapravatdumrong retrieved her slit lamp for Doctor Mason who began to examine Rennie's eyes. Of course she was no expert but knew that Rennie's cataracts were quite advanced and would easily show under the light. Try as she might, she could not find any evidence of cataracts in either eye. She asked Rennie to read her wall chart, and she was astounded to find her vision was, yes, perfect.

'What's wrong, doctor? What is happening to me?'

'I er...I'm not altogether sure, to be honest.' The doctor lowered her voice and spoke. ' Can you hear me, Rennie?'

'Yes, of course.'

'What is my name? Can you pronounce it for me.'

'I can remember your name Doctor Chevapravatdumrong.'

I would like to examine your ears, is that alright?' She retrieved her otoscope and looked in both ears. All was well. She took her blood pressure 120/60 perfect for a twenty year old. She asked Rennie to lift her knees as high as she could and found she had perfect articulation on lower and then upper limbs, no stiffness in her hands and fingers, which had lost their tell tale lumps and disfiguration.

The doctor sat back in her chair and reread her notes. 'How do I write this up?' she thought to herself, looking at Doctor Mason, who shook her head. 'Something for the practice meeting I think, Doctor,' she said leaving the room, a broad smile on her face.

'Do you know what's wrong doctor?'

'All I can find is what's right at the moment, Rennie.'

Outside, Rennie's doctor consulted with Mason, neither spoke for a few long moments. Meanwhile in the consulting room, Rennie was getting stressed and worried, reluctant to ask what it was that she now had.

'I think we should get her in for a range of tests. I want a full examination of her pre-existing conditions. We have a geriatric specialist contact at The London Teaching don't we? Doctor Sweet isn't it? She is an excellent physician.'

'Yes, let's do that.'

'And make sure you write these up, I want to report to the team meeting next Monday. See if you can get Mrs Sutcliffe in to see Doctor Sweet urgently and get a preliminary report from her.' With that Mason walked away, stopped a moment, looked down, shook her head slowly, then disappeared into her own room.

Doctor Chevapravatdumrong watched her colleague

disappear wondering what she should tell her patient. She sat back down opposite Rennie leaning forward in her chair and took one of her perfect hands. She could not believe that all evidence of disease was gone, even so she continued to hold her hand as she spoke.

'Rennie, there is nothing to concern yourself about. Doctor Mason and I are in agreement on that. We would like you to go to the London Hospital and see a colleague of ours who will have another look and see what's going on. Can I ask, have you been feeling faint since last week?'

'Yes, this morning. A bit light headed. Dizzy, you know?'

'OK, I am going to ask you to stop taking you blood pressure pills for a while until you have seen Doctor Sweet in London, alright? In fact stop taking all your medication until you see her.'

'Yes. Can I ask – am I going to be all right, Doctor.'

'I have a feeling for some reason, you are alright, right now. I'll call you tomorrow with your appointment, we'll get you in quickly. But please don't worry. You're fine. Call me if you are still worried.'

Doctor Chevapravatdumrong wrote up her notes carefully, showing them to Doctor Mason and the practice team who confirmed the findings of their examinations.

'Please don't say anything of this to anyone other than the practice physicians. I have a feeling this might be the subject of controversy. I don't know what it is that has happened to Rennie. It is all very, well...strange.'

It seemed that Rennie's agues and illnesses had just disappeared, literally overnight. Her eyesight, hearing, blood pressure, all her many and varied chronic conditions had of themselves just – disappeared. She had the health and vigour of a twenty year old inside a body of an eighty-three year old.

Croydon Beach

And there it was. After all the examinations and questions and enquiries. After the research of medical journals and peer reviews, it could not be understood. Rennie Sutcliffe was a medical phenomenon. It seems one morning she awoke to find she was cured of all her ills. But little would the doctors realise it was not the blessing anyone would have wished for.

When Doctor Chevapravatdumrong saw Rennie three weeks later, following her consultation with the geriatric specialist, Doctor Sweet, she explained as fully as she was able, their medical deliberations. Once done, she noted that despite her seeming medical miracle she was uncharacteristically downhearted.

'But Rennie, excuse me for asking, surely this is all very good news for you, is it not? Aren't you feeling fine?'

'Well, yes and no doctor.'

'But why is it not?' she asked.

'I have lost my friends. '

'You have lost your friends? But why?' Doctor Chevapravatdumrong was non-plussed.

'Well we used to talk about all our ailments and such, it seemed it was what kept us together. I just don't seem to have anything much in common with each other anymore.'

Doctor Chevapravatdumrong leaned back in her chair. Surely, she thought, anyone would want to be in Rennie's situation.

'Can you help me doctor, please?'

'I don't understand Rennie. What do you think I can do about what has happened? You are fit and healthy and I am a doctor?'

'I wonder, please, could you put everything back the way it was before.'

Croydon Beach

Mr Jeffers Dreams his Build House

'There is a pleasure in the pathless woods,
There is a rapture on the lonely shore,
There is society, where none intrudes
by the deep sea, and music in its roar...'

'There, that should do her.' He was pleased with the inspiring words that would define his project. Mr Jeffers sat back, reading and rereading the pinned note above his desk. 'Perfect. Now it begins,' he assured himself, 'let's do it,' he exclaimed, punching the air then wincing as his arm went into spasm. 'Maybe better not do that again though,' he informed himself, vigorously rubbing and rotating his shoulder. He glowed as once more he read his words.

'My own shore, my own woods and society, and none will intrude, not even in the planning stage.' His secret plans were being laid. It would take a while to see them completed, but he would dedicate as much time as he was able, to see it through to the end.

'After all,' he told himself, ' what else am I doing? Watching too much TV or 'Trying to find lots of things not to do'.' He happily hummed the old Bing Crosby tune.

Mrs Jeffers had tried to engage and distract him, trying to enthuse him with decorating the kitchen or refurbishing the bathroom – again. But he figured the kitchen and the bathroom, like all the other rooms in their house, had already taken up too much of his life; having decorated nearly all of them at least twice, sometime,

Croydon Beach

three times, since they moved there all those years and decades ago.

Mr Jeffers unnecessarily straightened the note, wondering whether he should leave such a clue to his plans in plain sight of Mrs Jeffers. 'It's just a few lines of poetry,' he mused, 'what conclusions could she draw from that? I'll leave it there, for daily inspiration.' He also copied and pasted Byron's poem to the top of the title page of his project workbook, encrypted the file and saved it. Every time he opened the folder it would be the first thing he would see, helping to keep his mind focussed on the purpose of his project. In the short time since he had decided on his project, he had become more relaxed. He felt himself smile more; a smile from his youth and which he thought he would never feel again. He strode to the shops with an exaggerated enthusiasm for this simplest of daily tasks; eager to return and take up the project once again.

He had heard Byron's lines two months before on BBC radio 4's Poetry Please, where listeners request their favourite verses to be read out on air. Not known previously for liking poetry he had fallen in love with the words, and more importantly with its meaning for him. Thus inspired and unbeknownst to his wife, Mr Jeffers would plan out the whole thing and execute it in total secrecy, seeing it through to the end.

'She wouldn't understand. She would think it's just more of my moans and complaints about the house,' he kept telling himself. It was true: Mrs Jeffers had stopped listening to his inner yearning to be away from their current house some twenty years before. He longed to live somewhere else, away from familiarity and reminders of all its contempts for a life not lived but merely allowed to pass by. She would not entertain any idea of moving, happy as she was where they had lived all those years of their marriage and before; even if Mr Jeffers had grown to increasingly despise what it meant to him and

Croydon Beach

expressed his contempt for the street and its locality.

'Inertia,' his inner monologue informed him, 'settling for what is familiar and cosy and boring; meanwhile life outside goes on all around you. As my good friend Bobby D sings.'

'Look,' she would tell him each time he brought up the subject, 'we have worked long and hard on this house to make it what it is. We have friends around and just where would we move to, tell me that? What would we do at our age in a new area? How would we make new acquaintances?' And on the list of questions would go. It wasn't that they couldn't afford to buy another place, it was just that that couldn't agree on the need to give up all their settled comfort, up all their sticks they had and move somewhere else and start again. And so Mr Jeffers slowly disappeared under the counterweight of Mrs Jeffers' reasoning. All of which he understood, of course. Her reluctance for change dwelled snugly within the conservative and shrinking realm of age.

After their last discussion on the matter, some four years before, Mr Jeffers had sworn never to broach the subject again. What would be the point? Mrs Jeffers could not be moved; would not be moved, in any direction. Over those years he had slowly withdrawn into his shell; each day rising to look out of the windows at all the familiar vistas and would close his eyes to visualise a fantasy forest, through the trees, along unbeaten paths, hoping to emerge into some imagined scene of mountains, with a distant lake perhaps, shimmering in the early morning light, drawing him ever closer to its heart. Then he would envision himself at the top of a high hill looking across a verdant valley, spread his arms wide, throwing his head back he would spin and spin through all its cardinals of the compass until he was dizzy with it all... Then reality would bite. From along the street and into his ears would invade the sounds of the daily traipse of parents taking their squalling children to school, then thirty minutes later trailing back to examine what remained of their days, before returning six hours later on the reverse cycle, thence to be repeated over and over again, generation after generation. There was no escape. And so, if any casual passer-by happened to glance up, they might have caught Mr Jeffers standing with his eyes firmly shut and an oblique, almost rapturous smile on his face, arms outstretched, his head tossed back day-dreaming and in full flight. But this was less likely in these times of smart phones when passers-by only looked down into their phones and rarely did they even glance up to see where they were going. And in Mr Jeffers' opinion, they weren't going anywhere; only, where their phones took them.

Upon opening his eyes from his reverie, the first thing he would see were the houses opposite, which, since he had moved into the street forty years before, had spawned two generations of children. He had spied them being push-chaired up and down the street, watched as grandparents visited, got greyer and died. Saw the children going to school, their first cars, girlfriends, a wedding. He had become the reluctant voyeur, watching the narrow Edwardian street, with its tidy hunched-together houses, as over the years it had slowly filled with parked cars, despising their ugliness as they sat in the curb, under the yellow street lights. But despite all his protestations and pleading, his wife was still reluctant to move, and Mr Jeffers wallowed in his unhappiness until he became resigned to his ultimate destiny of dying in a place he despised.

To the rear of his small house, he would look each day at the small handkerchief garden he had modelled and remodelled several times, now overgrowing. He had told Mrs Jeffers that he wanted to rewild it, let the lawn grow, let weeds attend the beds amongst old bulbs and unpruned shrubs. But in truth he just could not be bothered any more,. If Mrs Jeffers wanted to take over as chief gardener, she was welcome to do so. Long before he had given up on decorating the house for the same reason. DIY had gone the same way. Mrs Jeffers would try to engage him, but would end quietly enraging him.

'What's that dear? Sorry, I wasn't er…'

'I said, do you think we should decorate the bathroom?'

'When was the last time we er…?' Then he remembered the four times he and she had redecorated the bathroom. After he had re-plumbed the whole room when they had first moved in.

'Five years ago. It's looking really shabby, dear.'

Is it?' he would rejoin, distantly. Then after a pause, Mrs Jeffers would continue.

So, what do you think?' He knew this was ritual, knew the form and process of this line of questioning. As a bathroom it functioned well, but as an ageing trophy room it lacked impact.

'Then yes, why not,' he replied getting back to his favourite subscribed Youtube channel: 'Build an off grid cabin for $4000.' Mr Jeffers knew the interrogation would not end there. He steeled himself.

'OK. Any ideas about colours? Should we get a new suite? What about…' And he would drift away trying not to think of colour charts; types of finish; miserable plumbers; reluctant builders; and sloppy painters; all of whom would need monitoring and watching and, of course paying; the tedium of patronising their foibles, and their quirky builder ways in order to 'keep in with them'. And of course there were the days when they wouldn't turn up, and when they did the endless mugs of sugary bloody tea, always the tea. Mr Jeffers did not want to know any more about any of it.

Croydon Beach

'I am happy with whatever you decide, dear,' he would reply. 'Go right ahead.' Just don't involve me, was his unspoken coda.

At this Mrs Jeffers, would look askance at Mr Jeffers and express a deep sigh of frustrated exhaustion, then inevitably walk from the room muttering something about relationships, trying to get a reaction. It had usually worked, but he had learned not to follow up; Mr Jeffers was done. Life for him now was a slow running down of the curtain, sitting in his chair, in what he considered his two up two down pine box. He had no ambition, no prospect and no purpose, and in that way he felt free of all responsibility to himself, his wife and to the universe. He was stuck, mired in a history of his own making of inertia and inaction; he had no one else to blame – it was his fault. He was an outline sketch, with old age rubbing away at the edges of what remained, slowly erasing all traces of his paltry existence; a cartoon with about as much substance; uncoloured by events and experiences of a life fully lived fading with the age of days.

Yet, he still wasn't happy just to let things drift away. He was less unhappy when he dreamed of a house far away from that road, its inhabitants and its dull predictable familiarity. But that was that, he bowed to the inevitability of life out his control; stuck fast following a routine of domesticity and a regimen of prescription drugs and medical appointments. He had pawned his life cheaply, lost the ticket somewhere down all those years, leaving no possibility of redemption.

*

That was until that late Sunday night, in bed with his ear tucked next to the radio listening to Roger McGough and waiting for sleep. McGough was introducing listeners favourite poems when, on the

Croydon Beach

edge of sleep, Mr Jeffers heard Byron's Childe Harold's Pilgrimage. Suddenly he was wide awake and could not sleep wanting to hear it again. He struggled, moving around the bed trying to find his spot which always offered at least a few hours undisturbed sleep, but it would not be found. Three hours later, leaving Mrs Jeffers to her gentle snoring, he rose quietly from the bed. Still pyjamad and in his dressing gown, he padded down to the study. Online he looked up the poem and reread it, time and time again, until it was memorised. Falling immediately in love with its sentiment, it seemed to express for him everything he was feeling about his life. He hand wrote the lines and pinned them to the board above his desk, and stared at them for what seemed like hours.

He awoke in his chair, shivering as the sun was just coming up over the empty factory car park to the rear of the garden. He got up from his study chair and walked into the garden and through the thin trees, watched as the streaks of pink light began to wash the distant sky. To Mr Jeffers it had never looked so beautiful. Hope swelled in his chest, he felt alive again.

He would do it, he would dream his build house.

'Byron is right – a society where none intrudes,' he told that early morning sky, 'Yes, it's true, you don't need people to be in society,' he kept telling himself during those difficult early days of getting his secret plans into some sort of order. 'Dreaming was all well and good, but to make it come true and make it real you have to put in the hard yards. 'Hmm, I wonder if that should be metres? That's a point.' He made a note as he was used to imperial measures, should he switch to metric? It would help when it came to the plumbing, as he knew that all pipe work was in metric measurement.

*

Croydon Beach

Then what should he call his new home? It was a puzzler. 'Give it a name,' he told himself. 'To give something a name, is to confer on it life, a life it could never possess anonymously. He hadn't even considered what he would call it, until then it didn't seem too important. It would not have a number, no, numbers are for towns, streets and roads, but a name, individual and unique.

'Shangri-la, was a bit hackneyed; Theroux's Walden, too derivative; Butler's' Erehwon didn't express his feeling of location, nowhere backwards didn't really do it for him. He had given up on Utopia at the first thought. All these imagined world's, thought Mr Jeffers, it seems he wasn't the first to be struck by the idea. He had already scratched out the Mon Repos and Chez Nous cliches. But slowly in his mind the house began to construct itself, maybe he should wait and name it like launching a ship? It would be far away from the Madding crowd, from the street he and Mrs Jeffers had lived in for nearly forty years.

To Mrs Jeffers' consternation, Mr Jeffers had increasingly taken to talking to himself, mostly discussing things with some other, his other. Or furiously writing or sketching something. She would sometimes walk into a room where he had his draughtsman's drawing board out and hear him talking as if someone else were with him, in actual conversation, and usually to a background music of Elgar's Chanson de Matin or Beethoven's Pastoral Symphony.

'You are coming along fine. Just you wait. I'll make you a beauty. My creation.'

Answering questions he himself had asked.

'Shall I put you there? No, pride of place I think. There. How's that, now?'

'What's that, my love?' she would ask, overhearing when

Croydon Beach

passing the door left slightly open. She would look in. 'Were you calling me?'

'Oh, nothing. Sorry, I didn't hear you there,' and he would cover up the board as she entered. 'Just talking to myself, as you do.' And he would employ his dismissive smile from long ago, that one she had found so charming in their early days, now employed in a strange and worrying way.

'So, what's going on there?' she asked pointing at the covered drawing board, with its set and tee squares, his collection of mapping Rotring pens and coloured inks sitting alongside: his old and almost redundant draughting equipment inherited from his father, dug from the loft, dusted off and re-engaged for this important project He was drawing out the structure for a detailed three-dimensional 1/20th scale model of his house.

'What are you working on? Seems to have really captured your interest?' He slowly pulled over a covering sheet so that Mrs Jeffers could not see what it was he was working on.

'Er, nothing much. Just messing about really.' But he had no intention of showing Mrs Jeffers his plans. It was his house and his alone, and he would live there, alone; a society in nature where none, not even Mrs Jeffers, would intrude. Mrs Jeffers had expressed no desire to move, so any reference to a new house would, he knew, be met by quiet resignation, or annoyed irritation that the subject was raised yet again. As soon as it was completed, he was moving out and into his newly designed home. He would even make plans for removals and solicitors; arrange for builders and surveyors; everything down to the finest of details. It would be set in its own tiny grounds and garden. A terrace to open out to a short stroll to the lake. He would light the house. All areas would be accessed via a removable roof. Miniature furniture and furnishings would complete

Croydon Beach

his simple, uncluttered home.

'I said, you seem much taken with it, your latest project, is it? Will I be able to see what it is?' She was trying so hard to engage with her husband and felt she was losing him, or perhaps he was losing himself. This project of his was his first in years, and he seemed totally absorbed by it, perhaps even obsessed or possessed by it. She was being shut out, and that worried her. They had shared everything over their many years together; this was something new from Mr Jeffers.

'Yes, of course. I'll give you a peek when its done. I'd rather you didn't see it until it's finished. I want it to be a surprise. Still a lot to do. Maybe another year.'

'A year. Goodness.' And with that she left the room. Because of Mrs Jeffers' curiosity, he had taken to hiding his sketches and plans, rolling them up at the end of each session and placing them in a tube stowing them well out of sight under some furniture or some such. The emerging model was hidden amongst his older abandoned projects, emerging when she left the house when he could work unsuspected on the model. He grinned at the title he had written in the cardboard container that stored his drawings – MyTube.

Yes, he had indeed become obsessed and Mrs Jeffers was both concerned and relieved. Concerned that he seemed to be completely overtaken by his project and at the same time somewhat relieved that he no longer sat on the sofa trying desperately to find things to watch on YouTube and other subscribed TV channels.

The covid lockdowns had taken its toll on many people, but with his extra health vulnerabilities both he and Mrs Jeffers were completely isolated, rarely going beyond the boundaries of their small house. Boundaries which Mr Jeffers would patrol daily; a caged lion who had slowly lost his roar, as Mrs Jeffers had told her friends

Croydon Beach

on Zoom: she was worried. Then suddenly, and to her relief, he had found a new meaning to his life. She hadn't known exactly what it was, but as he had become so fragile, disturbing his new found positive equilibrium might push him back into his sullen moods.

Mrs Jeffers would Zoom meet with her friends and discuss Mr Jeffers' new found and increasingly obsessive behaviour; his disinterest in things, rarely leaving the house that he had professed a disliking for. She had ask her friends whether she should be concerned for her husband.

To her closest friend Linda, she confided how he had become moody and remote, hardly talked to her, but to himself more and more. He had no friends online, or anyone he talked to on the telephone. She tried to convey how seriously worried she was.

Doctor should be her first port of call, Linda had suggested. Maybe there's something going on more than just moodiness? Perhaps with the lockdown and everything, he is depressed, perhaps even a little… there was a pause as Linda sought the most diplomatic word; confused.

Mrs Jeffers all too well understood the code; Alzheimer's, that awful word, so loaded with meaning. But she explained that in the last month or so, he seemed to smile a lot, sing to himself and his appetite had improved. But he still would not talk to her about what was going on in that brain of his.'

To lighten the mood, Linda had suggested that perhaps he had found himself a fancy woman? At this they both laughed, imagining Mr Jeffers stepping out with another woman, it was of course totally out of the question. But he did have a mistress of an altogether different sort.

A holiday was suggested, something which Mrs Jeffers had already put to Mr Jeffers, but he would not be drawn away from his project. Whilst Mr Jeffers considered consulting their doctor, Mr Jeffers continued with his build house. Unlike their current house, his house would have the barest minimum of clutter. A kitchen table; two chairs; one easy chair and reading light; something for music; lots of bookshelves though, he would not skimp on that, and a sofa for relaxing after a hard day in his huge garden. He would have rooms to breathe. He looked away from the drawing board and stared at Byron's words in front of him and smiled widely.

'Rooms to breathe,' he sighed, as he began to glue the edges of the tiny main room together.

Whilst they were drying he thrashed out plans and costs; dimensions and of course location; builders and schedule of works. Drainage was a particularly contentious issue. The house would be off grid as would be gas and electricity. It would be a sustainable house, independent as much as possible. The roof would be solar panelled, geothermal heat pumps would provide heating in the fully insulated house with its triple glazed windows.

When his house was finished, he would walk around it, explore its spaces, examine its carefully crafted contours and detail. When sleep eluded him, lying in his wakefulness, he would quietly remove himself to his kitchen, make a hot drink and take it out on the night terrace, bundled against the cold and sit and watch the stars circling him as a Night Jar called from a large oak that dominated his view to the large wooded garden; at least that is how he imagined it to be. Tomorrow night, should he still be awake he would follow the gravel path leading down to a small lake, with a sandy shore, near which he had tied a small boat to the short jetty he'd had constructed there. Perhaps, depending on how his midnight mood would take him, when he had finished his hot chocolate, he would stroll down there and maybe take her out, so one day he decided, come what may, he

Croydon Beach

would.

*

His works schedule for the build was realistic. He began a project calendar, showing time lines, overlaps of schedules for the various trades. He found the names of several off the shelf house kits which could be altered to meet his highly specific specifications. Maybe he would buy the plot of land with an older property which he would apply to demolish using a similar foot print on which to build the new structure, a brown field site, in keeping with his personal environmental credentials.

'Can we talk?' Mrs Jeffers was becoming increasingly concerned. He had become quieter over the last few months, as the end approached, taking less interest in their mutual interests of cooking, walking and visiting theatres and art exhibitions. When he wasn't working on the house, he and Mrs Jeffers had taken to visiting RHS gardens, with him making notes; going to talks on landscaping and rewilding of gardens and the ecological sustainability of cottage gardens; composting and of earth closets. Mrs Jeffers was no longer relieved by his new found enthusiasms, but worried by his obsessions.

'Sorry dear, what was that?' asked Mr Jeffers.

'I'm worried about you.'

'Worried, why?'

'You've become, well, you've become a little, well, strange.'

'Strange? Strange how?'

'You don't... Well, you don't...'

'Don't what, dear?'

'Like now. You don't seem to here a lot of the time. Like you are constantly daydreaming. On one long revery. But it seems you are always in them these days.'

'It's the medication. They said it could have odd effects. Remember?'

Of course his wife remembered.

'The longer he is on the meds, he will seem a little strange, perhaps increasingly so. But it is preferable than for him to find himself increasingly forgetful and vague. These are powerful drugs, and you must try to understand that it is in the better of two distinct worlds he finds himself,' Mr Jeffers' specialist had told her, whilst Mr Jeffers was out of the consulting room.

But Mr Jeffers no longer felt had a need of his medication and had ceased taking them since the beginning of his project. 'I have my own drug,' he told himself.

Mrs Jeffers, despite all her efforts and with help from her friends and the doctors could not discover the source of Mr Jeffers obsession. Not until, that is, it was far too late.

*

Mr Jeffers, his build house finally completed, jangled his keys, stared briefly down at them then tossed them away. What need had he of keys? He looked up at the front door, then opened it stepping over the threshold and scanned the room before disappearing inside and closing the door behind him. He was happy.

Mr Jeffers is now in a home of a different sort than that which he had so fully and creatively imagined – locked in and roaming its rooms, its gardens and grounds, where none would intrude.

Mrs Jeffers visits less frequently than she used to. Mr Jeffers can sometimes hear someone knocking at the door, but he never answers, happy as he was to be alone. Sometimes they call at the windows, but

Croydon Beach

they soon get discouraged and move away. Now, the day long, he sits in the chair he imagined by the fire he invented, looking from the window he created, across the field to his lake he had conjured, surrounded by trees and framed by the Malvern Hills. So ensconced, he watches the sun go down over the factory buildings across the car park of the residential home in Islington, as the evening chorus trills and echoes in his ears.

The model of the build house that Mr Jeffers dreamed can still be found should anyone trouble themselves to look. Dust covered and abandoned it sits in a dark corner of the loft. And if, on some quiet night or in the silent suffused early hours of the morning, finding it, you should look into one of its tiny cellophane windows you might see Mr Jeffers standing, staring, a smile fixed on his face; a smile from his youth and which he thought he would never feel again. His head now filled with the remainder of Byron's poem, which he would keep repeating to the chagrin of carers and others around him, but which was a source of some small comfort to Mrs Jeffers:

'...I love not man the less, but nature more.'

The Bookseller's Temptation

A warm, late spring afternoon in April 2001, Sainte Colombe, Southern France; market day. Stalls are spread around the ancient and charming town square. Fresh vegetables and fruit colour the scene like a Monet painting. The cries of the sellers trouble the usually quiet square, promising delights of home grown produce direct from small farms and gardens. Cheeses, spices, fresh horse flesh and live poultry perfume the air. Shoes, handbags, table cloths and bed linen, cellophaned neatly festoon tables and stalls, whilst heavy ladies undergarments, stays and corsets swing from their hooks, twisting in the light breeze, like the ghastly remains of gibbeted prisoners.

The day finds Marcel DuGrippe as he squats on a stool hunched behind a small table. He is in his mid fifties, but looks sixty. The *moustache grise* hides the whole of his top lip; prematurely grey and unkept it hangs and hides his mouth that continually makes seeming small nervous chewing movements, but which are in fact a convocation of curses and prayers. The curses are for the stallholders; the prayers for those who pass by his table, impervious to what he offers – the glory of salvation and the love of the Lord. And the man is at war with himself. He sees sin everywhere, and worries for its consequences, wondering at the false delights and distractions and what they might possibly hold for the sinners; he troubled to find any reason for their peccadillos and could find none, save the continuing poisonous intervention by the Dark One. He knew this was Satan's world, which surrounded him; he was the only one who showed the light of love and redemption in Apollyon's realm. Inside this little man offering his bibles and payer books is violent turmoil, all priceless. Like a muslim child learning the Koran, this violence in his breast, makes him rock back and forth behind his green baize card table, upon which sits his six or seven bibles and several prayer books. One bible stands propped and held open by a piece of misted plastic; showing verses which to him are apposite for that day and that day's shoppers. Should anyone pause to read the open text, he would not move or speak, the Word would do that for him. He was the bringer of The Good News and not its originator. Of course, should the curious person want any more information he would give it, at least that which was in his humble gift to provide, but this had never happened in all the days of his coming there, no one asked.

At the early beginning of each market day, in his apartment, DuGrippe would prepare for his lonely vigil with fasting and prayer. And being a devout Christian he felt it beholden of him to offer the faith he had received through the grace of his Saviour to whomsoever could be persuaded to listen. He had never been a religious man, not being associated to any church, or ever wanted to be, but followed his own precepts to proselytise his own interpretations of the Word.

Almost wholly friendless in his piety, DuGrippe wasn't an easy man in conversation. He averred the companionship to be found at his village's *tabac*, or in the PMU bar, with its horse racing and lottery. These places he foreswore as palaces of wild debauchery and bedevilment. Village life was not for him. Not even the spiritual comforts of the 14th Century church and its congenial priest. A few polite words with the counter staff at the *boulangerie* or the *boucherie* was all he would exchange; taking home his meagre purchases, before settling to read from the Book of Everlasting Life. Home was a place for prayer and contemplation, the world was where the evil one stalked his prey amongst the already damned.

DuGrippe hadn't always been such a recluse. Many years before he had a young fiancé and a wedding planned. That was until she'd had second thoughts, handed back his ring and took up with a farmer's son from the next village whom she had met at a dance, to which DuGrippe had escorted her. In his bitter disappointment, the consolations of his few friends offered scant recompense for his loss, over which he grieved for more than a year. It was this singular event that drove him into the welcoming arms of Jesus. Prior to his doomed relationship his interest in spiritual matters was close to nothing; after it he slowly came to realise that this was his way in a wicked world. A world where promises meant nothing, being of such little value, that trampling the hearts of those who professed their love were as nothing. The Devil walked the land entering the souls of all, it was easy work for the Dark One.

And so had DuGrippe foresworn the world of Mammon, consumerism and all its perfidious trickeries, and became an ascetic, living alone, wanting no one, minding none. He read The Bible and learned every verse, could quote directly without recourse to the book itself; he was a walking, breathing bible. There was only one truth and only one place for him – The Bible. To this end he had set about producing his own. Like the monastic scribes of the middle ages, each was fully handwritten, illuminated and personalised, from Genesis to Revelations; each taking many months of concentrated work to complete. When they were sold at the market he would be sure that once his words had been read, a soul would set on the right and righteous path to their own personal salvation.

And so it was, like a religious ritual, and no matter the time of year or the weather, the morning of market day became the most important day for him. Before setting off for Sainte Colombe, he would pray for an hour or so, then load his 50cc Mobylette motorcycle panniers with a few personalised bibles and prayer books; a bottle of his own well water; strap to his back a small worn card table and fold-up fishing stool, and ride the long ride from his village to the town's market square. He would always be the first stallholder to arrive, quickly setting his table and arraying his books. As he did this, for each bible he carefully laid out, he imagined a damned soul reading the book, and a soul being saved; in advance of which event each market day he thanked the Almighty for His beneficence and the compassionate consolations of the Word.

As the sun rose over the market square and other stallholders slowly and cheerfully set out their offers, he would sit on his fold-up fishing stool and watch the day's activity unfold. Conversations rose and laughter filled the head of DuGrippe as he sat by his bibles. Every now and again he would move one slightly, or adjust the positions of his small pile of pamphlets which were to explain their meaning to the passersby, should they not wish to purchase one of the books without knowing their full purpose. These pamphlets he would have to keep from curling by shuffling the top faded ones to the bottom of the pile.

He spoke to no one, even though he was to be found there every market day, and he came to recognise those around him, but never asked or wanted to know their names. If they were more interested in Mammon rather than the true God, then he would have no counsel or conversation with them: those who passed by were already damned in his eyes, as surely, as they were in the Lord's. This inner certainty settled his mind. For each one who passed him by barely glancing at him, he would say a small prayer, or sometimes it would be a curse, depending on the mood he found himself in that day. His cynicism knew no bounds.

In the years that he had been on his mission at the market, he had never sold a single one of his bibles. Hardly anyone stopped to flick their pages or ask questions. He was there, that was all that counted, he was God's living presence, the physical embodiment of faith; he knew they would come, his faith was solid, his path certain.

This particular day, it is around twelve-thirty in the market and quiet. Everyone according to French tradition is eating their lunchtime repasts. During this sacred time, a few tourists straggle through gazing in wonder at the offerings that are so bereft in their own countries. The bible man is perched on his stool sipping warm water from an old soft drink bottle brought from home. The temperature is unseasonably hot and he has not an umbrella under which to shelter from the sun's heat. Still he sits uncomfortable and penitent, sweating, his head throbbing from dehydration. He imagined the fires of hell, a thousand times worse than what he was experiencing, and so for him, was bearable; he would not have to beat himself that evening; the sun's heat would suffice for that day's self flagellation for his contact with the spawn of the Dark One.

It was towards the end of the market's lunch, things were beginning to stir. Still he sat awaiting the Lord's revelation of his good works amongst the fallen. He was there should he be needed. He had his head down trying to avoid the post noon's heat, when at the front edge of his table there appeared the bottom of what must be a young woman. What should he do, trapped as he was behind his table? Should he ask her if she wanted anything? Could he help her? It seemed unlikely.

Here in front of him was Eve, progenitor of Man's Fall from God's grace. Should he reach out and move his sacred texts nearer and away from that backside. Why was she standing there? Could she not move? Still she stood her back to him, obviously she was not looking at his display. He started to sweat more in the increasing heat of this dilemma. Something was stirring in DuGrippe. What was this he was feeling? The temptation of this modern Eve began to rise in him. He closed his eyes tight, trying to squeeze out the thoughts that were welling inside him. 'Why doesn't she move?' he asked himself. 'Please god, in your mercy, please remove this temptation.' He began to pray as fervently as he had ever prayed.

For temptation it was; something he had resisted since coming to the Lord. Here was God's test and the Devil's work in the singular form of this young, brazen and shameless woman. 'Maybe when I open my eyes she will have gone.' Could he risk it? What if she was still there? Yet he must look, he could not keep his eyes shut forever.

Still with his head bowed, DuGrippe slowly began to open his eyes. Much to his relief the bottom was gone. He felt relief flow through him like a river of God's blessings. He knew on arriving home he would have to beat himself to excess for those thoughts put there by the devil. Beat them out of his body and his mind. Yes, that was the right way, the only way. The certainty that God had answered his prayer, was proof of His willingness to intervene in the lives of men of faith.

His head came slowly up ready to recommence his study of the passing sinners. Then he saw not two metres away, the girl, only now he could see all of her. She was slim, long-legged in tight shorts which served to emphasise their sinewy length; bared at the midriff and conscious of herself as she will be in no other time in her life. Wearing dark glasses, she looked for interest from others, trying out her display on the passers-by – her own personal display. She needs the reassurance of being wanted, desired for her physicality. Her shaded eyes scan for interest, that her presence is recognised, her beauty advertisement is drawing the interest of men and women – both desire and envy. She is opening like a new flower in the spring sunshine.

There is a purity in the moments that follow. The young woman, hardly old enough for that delineation, yet needing attention, needing the solace of interest from others, and needs must when the Devil himself drives. Turning, the girl notices the old man looking at her; and finding no other interest from the few passing men and boys, her eyes fix upon the old man's visage, as she in her turn returns his stare, and as she does, moves slowly back towards his table. Practising her smile on the old man, all the while finding his features and his demeanour disgusting to her. 'The old are revolting,' she thinks as she approaches. 'Look at him, wanting me, imagined his hands exploring my body and more. Loathsome creep.'

'Can I look?' she asks of the old man.

He nods in answer, it was all he could manage, as he looks away and down at the slim fingers which slowly pick up a bible and flicked through the pages, pretending to alight on some verse that interests her curiosity. He knows what she is doing, trying to do, this devil made flesh. She wants to lead him away from the light and into the darkness that dwells in her blackened soul.

Eventually his eyes return to the girl. Then he notices a bead of sweat making its listless way from her neck and into the chamber behind her thin blouse. Tiny hairs where the sweat has travelled glisten in the sun. Her head is still bent in her apparent pretence of reading the hand written scripture.

'I have never seen anything like this before. Who wrote this all out? Was it you?'

'Yes,' he replied as dismissively as he could manage.

'Are all these hand written?'

'Yes, they are.'

'But why? Why take the trouble to write the whole Bible out?'

'You wouldn't understand,' he replied reaching out to take the book from her.

She pulled it towards her and out of his reach, still amazed at what she was looking at.

'I mean like wow, y'know?' She pulled her sunglasses up to settle in her hair and continued to look through the book. 'How much is this one?'

He had no idea. He hadn't considered that they would ever be sold, that it was ever a possibility. Just his presence at the market was to be a reminder that an alternative life could be led, not by merely feeding bloated appetites and desires of the market's stalls. He held out his hand for the girl to give back the book.

'It's not for sale. You cannot buy what is in these books. What is in these books is free to anyone who has a pure heart and seeks truth.' He replaced the book alongside the others.

'So, if you are not selling why do you have a market stall? I mean seems a bit weird, don't you think?'

All of this was as much as he had said to anyone in a long while. He eyes fell to the edge of the table at the same level as the girl's pierced navel, sporting a ring and jewellery. He tried to look away from it but could not, he was stuck. Once again he beseeched the Lord for another timely intervention, praying for the girl to leave and leave him alone. The girl pulled her sunglasses back over her eyes and stared at the man.

'You really ought to sell those you know, I reckon they could get a good price.' With that the girl walked away. DuGrippe resettled himself trying not to relive what had just taken place. A little later a couple turned up at the table and asked to look at the unique hand scribed books.

'Our daughter told us of your manuscripts, could we perhaps look at one?'

DuGrippe examined the couple who had spawned a Jezebel, with no thought of how she was showing her wares in the market for all to see. Were they not ashamed, considered DuGrippe? Should he say something, rather than allow their sullied hands to despoil one of his precious bibles? But it was too late. The woman had picked up a book and was respectfully leafing though it as her husband looked admiringly over her shoulder at the illuminated work.

'Why this is marvellous. Truly wonderful,' they both agreed, looking up at the scribe. 'Is this all your own work?'

'It is,' he replied, holding out his hand to retrieve it.

'Our daughter said that they are not for sale. Is that right?'

DuGrippe nodded, replacing the book upon his table as far from their reach as possible. 'They are not for sale.'

'But surely you will take…'

'They are not for sale. Good afternoon to you.'

The couple started to walk away, then stopped. 'Are you sure you won't…?'

'Good afternoon.' He closed his eyes and they disappeared from his view. Give the Devil his due, thought DuGrippe, temptation took many forms and came in many guises. DuGrippe smiled at his ability to recognise all his wiles. Behind his closed eyes, DuGrippe said a silent prayer, asking the Lord forgiveness for his pride in thinking that anyone could be interested in his work dedicated to Him and to Him alone. He sweltered in the afternoon heat, grateful for the discomfort he felt that he would endure as his penance. After nodding off into a fitful, sweaty slumber, a shadow crossed in front of his eyes awakening him. He opened them to see a tall rotund figure standing before him, giving him some relief from the sun's heat. The sun was directly behind the man, shining around his head, almost like a halo from a religious picture.

DuGrippe, fresh from sleep, struggled to see who the man was, he did seem familiar. Eventually he revealed himself from shadow as the congenial priest from his village appeared at the table.

'I have just heard of your bibles,' said the priest, carefully turning the pages thick with colour and heavy with words. 'I hope you don't mind…' Would it matter if he did? These priests! 'Why this is marvellous, Monsieur,' said the priest. 'Simply astounding. One might even say, miraculous. How long did they take to copy and illustrate?' DuGrippe found the priest's voice soothing in a way he had never experienced before. Having only heard it once or twice before, it still seemed as if the voice did not belong to the priest at all, but to some ethereal presence; this feeling he put down to the heat and the thirst he was experiencing.

'I'm sorry Monsieur, you must be thirsty, are you not? Your voice sounds a little cracked.'

'Yes I am, but my bottle is dry and…'

The priest picked up the bottle and shook it. 'Seems full to me. Here.' And he removed the stopper and gave it to DuGrippe, who gratefully slaked his thirst, as he did so, occasionally looked at the bottle, which he was sure he had drunk dry some hours before.

'So you were saying how long each took,' asked the priest.

'About five months for each of them,' DuGrippe reluctantly offered, wiping his mouth, and still staring up at the face in shadow.

'Is this all you have, right here,' continued the intrigued priest.

'I have a dozen more at home,' DuGrippe replied without emotion.

'Goodness me! Astonishing. So you have been working on

these for…' the priest did a swift calculation. '…twelve and seven, times five… then divide by twelve,'

'Nearly eight years,' replied the little man.

'Astonishing. This is a true work of faith, and if I may say, individual works of art,' added the excited priest, still looking through the superb illuminations in the book. 'Please, I beg you, you must let me buy one from you. Just say how much. I would like to display it permanently in our church. Perhaps a different page according to the day for the congregation to read. I must say, acts of faith such as are on display here, are extremely rare in these times of godless Mammon, would you not agree?'

DuGrippe was caught. This was a man of faith before him, whom he would never have considered a true man of God, yet how could he deny him? What would Jesus do? Would he deny someone a bible for the third time; a Peter denying the Christ himself? But to sell, would be like the money changers in the temple. Would it not be in Mammon's name, the bankrupt god himself, to sell to the priest? He looked at the book the priest held. Then looked up.

'Please Curé, take one. I will not sell it.'

'But all your work, Monsieur,' replied the priest, looking at the book once more, then over at DuGrippe. 'surely you must place a very high a value upon it?'

'You already have, Curé,' DuGrippe replied, returning the pleased smile of the man standing way above him.

Beggar's Belief – Small Change

Reprise...

'Any change friend?' enquired the ever-hopeful beggar of the purposefully striding city man.

The man, for once overcoming his well honed reluctance to offer anything whatsoever to the voice from the empty shop doorway, glancingly observed:

'None at all,' he said, not missing a step. 'In fact, I'm still a greedy, selfish bastard; lock me up if you can.' And passed on down the street, smiling at his *bon mots*.

Although unseen by his disappearing interlocutor, the hopeful beggar returned the smile; his world was set back once more upon its proper axis. For the briefest of moments honesty had been restored to his city.

And then...

Away down the road, the master of the universe, on his way to the Futures Market just off Threadneedle street, began to slow his normal urgent pace. There was something about that beggar that had begun to trouble him. Of course he tried to push it from his mind, give the voice no thought, he had barely looked at the ragged bundle as he passed him by, and yet?

He had a long day ahead and it was a day to make money, a lot of money. He was a futures man, a trader in futures and a deal-maker. That bum at the side of the road represented everything he despised; if he really wanted to, he could do something about his pathetic situation. He picked up his pace, then slowed again. Something still nagged at him; what was it that was so familiar about that parasite? He stopped, looked at his watch, seven-thirty, he was already an hour late.

'Damn it!' he said to himself. And he turned back to the man; he wanted to get a good look at him. 'Who is he?' The Futures Market called to him, but the future could wait a while longer.

He arrived back at the shop doorway where the bum still sat wrapped in a duvet, a small dog at his side, which he stroked lovingly. Without looking up, he asked:

'Any change, friend?'

The futures man dug into his pocket and found a ten pence piece. 'Here.' He held it waiting for the face to reveal itself.

'Thanks. Have a nice day,' he said, examining the meagre coin he'd been given. His face came up and squinted at the Futures man, who staggered back in horror. There, unshaven, sun scorched, his hair lank and unruly, was the futures man's own face which stared back at him.

'Some change, huh?' said the voice in the doorway.

Printed in Great Britain
by Amazon